The insights provided by work in applied linguistics can be of genuine support to all teachers facing the many complex demands of language learning and teaching. The Penguin English *Introducing Applied Linguistics* series aims to provide short, clear and accessible guides to key topics – helping teachers to keep abreast of this rapidly developing field by explaining recent research and its relevance to common problems and concerns. The books are designed for practical use: they focus on recognizable classroom contexts, suggest problem-solving approaches, and include activities and questions for further study.

Introducing Applied Linguistics presumes an increasing convergence of interest among all English language teachers, and it aims to be relevant to both teachers of English as a second or foreign language and to teachers of English as a mother tongue. As the relationship between linguistics and language teaching continues to develop, so the need grows for books which introduce the field. This series has been developed to meet that need.

The words that appear in **bold** type are
explained in the glossary.

Acknowledgements

Whilst acknowledging many influences in the writing of this book, I must emphasize the debt that I owe particularly to Ron Carter and to John Harris, without whose help, support and guidance this book would never have been written. My thanks are primarily directed to you both.

I would also like to mention my recent colleagues who have also 'had a say' in its writing: Steve Anwyl, Jenny Cobley, Julie Ferreday, Roy Goddard, Pat Seymour, Lindy Stone and Jack Todhunter.

Finally, thanks to the enthusiasm and committment of Linda Cotton, Mick Connell, Andy Heard, and Guy Merchant.

The publishers make grateful acknowledgement to the following for permission to reproduce copyright material: extract from *a speech at the presentation of the Thomas Cranmer Prize*, by His Royal Highness The Prince of Wales, December 1989; *Mountain Language*, by Harold Pinter, Faber and Faber Ltd, 1991; *Blitz*, by Mark Honingsbaum, The Guardian, September 1991; *Rates of Exchange*, by Malcolm Bradbury, Secker and Warburg, 1983; *The Language of Children and Adolescents*, by S. Romaine, Basil Blackwell Ltd, 1984; *User Guide to NB300 Research Machine*, Research Machines plc, 1992; *A guessing game starts*, by Bob Westerdale, The Sheffield Star, March 1994; *Revenge of the Lawn*, by Richard Brautigan, Simon and Schuster, 1971, by permission of Ianthe Brautigan Swensen; *The Plain English Story*, Plain English Campaign, 1986; *The Patriot* from *Latter Day Psalms*, by Nissim Ezekiel, Oxford University Press, 1982

For a full list of references, please see page 112.

Penguin Books
Introducing Standard English

Jeff Wilkinson is a senior lecturer in English and Education and works in the Centre for English in Education at Sheffield Hallam University. He has extensive experience of initial and in-service teacher training at both primary and secondary levels and has a particular interest in language study and its relationship to the development of reading and writing skills. He is co-author (with John Harris) of *Reading Children's Writing* (Unwin Hyman, 1986) and *In the Know: a Guide to English Language in the National Curriculum* (Stanley Thornes, 1990). He is currently researching the relationship between knowledge about language and the teaching of grammar in primary and secondary schools.

Ronald Carter is Professor of Modern English Language in the Department of English Studies at the University of Nottingham. He is the author of many books on applied linguistics and was the National Co-ordinator for the LINC (Language in the National Curriculum) project from 1989 to 1992.

David Nunan is Professor of Applied Linguistics and Director of the English Centre at the University of Hong Kong. He has worked as a TESOL teacher, teacher educator, curriculum designer and materials writer and consultant in Britain and overseas and is the author of many books on applied linguistics and ELT.

Other Titles in the Series

Introducing

STANDARD ENGLISH

Jeff Wilkinson

Series Editors:
Ronald Carter and David Nunan

PENGUIN
ENGLISH

PENGUIN ENGLISH

Published by the Penguin Group
Penguin Books Ltd, 27 Wrights Lane, London W8 5TZ, England
Penguin Books USA Inc., 375 Hudson Street, New York, New York 10014, USA
Penguin Books Australia Ltd, Ringwood, Victoria, Australia
Penguin Books Canada Ltd, 10 Alcorn Avenue, Toronto, Ontario, Canada M4V 3B2
Penguin Books (NZ) Ltd, 182–190 Wairau Road, Auckland 10, New Zealand

Penguin Books Ltd, Registered Offices: Harmondsworth, Middlesex, England

First published 1995
1 3 5 7 9 10 8 6 4 2

Typeset by Datix International Limited, Bungay, Suffolk
Printed in England by Clays Ltd, St Ives plc
Filmset in 10/13 pt Monophoto Times

Contents

Contents

Introduction

Consider the approaches offered to the teaching of Standard English in the following textbooks currently available for use in primary and secondary schools in England and Wales. The first extract is from a series of English textbooks for pupils in primary schools called *Exploring Language* (Lutrario 1993):

The following activities will heighten children's awareness of the nature and forms of Standard English:

1. **More than one**
   We are going to learn about how some words change to show whether they are singular (about one thing) or plural (about more than one thing).

2. **Past, present and future**
   We are going to learn about how verbs change to describe what happens in the past, the present and the future.

3. **He, she, it**
   We are going to learn about using pronouns.

The second extract is taken from a textbook for secondary-school pupils called *Language Links* (Sweetman 1990):

Today, Standard English is still the variety of English that is used for writing. For most people, this means writing down something that is different from their own speech. The mixture of Standard English and other dialects which most of us speak is rarely used in writing ... Standard English is the variety of English which you will need to use for most of the writing you do.

The teaching of Standard English in primary and secondary schools is rapidly becoming an area of concern, but, on the evidence of these two extracts, it is only vaguely, and intuitively, understood. The primary-school textbook sees the concept as a series of grammatical points, taught through decontextualized exercises, whereas the secondary-school textbook appears to take it as read that we all know what Standard English is, and where it is used.

This book attempts to explore more specifically the precise nature of Standard English and to relate such a description to the teaching of English in primary and secondary schools. The book considers the following topics:

1. <u>Introduction:</u> This chapter presents a view of Standard English from a historical perspective and explores attitudes to such a concept through the ages. It also concentrates on studying language uses in context.

2. <u>Standard English and standards of English</u> outlines attitudes to the notion of Standard English, based on prejudice and a lack of accurate description. It considers what Standard English actually is, and looks at the many aspects of English (spoken and written; Standard and non-Standard; accent and dialect).

3. <u>English and Other Englishes</u> considers Standard English more specifically in terms of regional, national and international forms. The focus here is more on the teaching of English as a second/foreign language.

4. <u>It ain't what you say</u> considers further the speech/writing differences evident in Standard English and looks at the implications for teachers.

5. <u>Reflecting on Language Use</u> outlines practical classroom activities for developing an awareness among students of the styles, purposes and variety of spoken and written Standard and non-Standard English.

6. <u>Assessing Standard English</u> focuses on the problems of assessing student performance and places the definitions of spoken

and written Standard English within the more general context of textual organization, as well as indicating some vocabulary and grammatical differences.

7. <u>Conclusion</u> emphasizes the complexity and variety of Standard English, and the need for teachers to establish common assumptions about its nature.

This book is designed to be both introductory and interactive. It is introductory in that it tries to describe the complexities of what is too often regarded as a matter of 'simple common sense'. It is interactive by including, at certain points in each chapter, activities designed to help the reader (or 'group' of readers) to reflect on the issues in question.

Above all, it is the hope of this book that any investigation of Standard English will help to broaden, not narrow, approaches to the production of both spoken and written English. 'All my proposals – that students should write in a variety of forms, that they should develop abilities in speech and drama, that they should read new works from different cultures – would bring about new collaborations and cooperations, new extensions of sympathy and imagination. We should transform our students from passive consumer to active maker' (Cox 1989). It is the 'active maker' of meaning and communication of English in specific contexts that this book is anxious to promote.

1 Introducing Standard English

Looking at the way English is used in our popular newspapers, our radio and television programmes, even in our schools and theatres, they [a great many people] wonder what it is about our country and our society that our language has become so impoverished, so sloppy and so limited – that we have arrived at such a dismal wasteland of banality, cliché and casual obscenity.

The Prince of Wales, December 1989

In this chapter we begin by examining attitudes to **Standard** English, which are an important aspect of debates concerning Standard English and its teaching. Some definitions of Standard English are indeed based on attitudes to language that are very deeply felt and maintained with considerable vigour.

1.1 Attitudes to language

ACTIVITY

Examine the following sentences. Decide which of them are examples of Standard English. Rank the sentences according to the degree to which they conform to your concept of Standard English.

1a

1. *She is in Leeds, but her family are in Manchester.*
2. *They went skiing. One of them slipped and bust his leg.*
3. *This is the woman of whom I was speaking.*

(Author's data)

Results from tests conducted with a hundred undergraduate students in 1993 indicate that sentence 3 is preferred as the sentence which most clearly conforms to Standard English. Sixty-four per cent of informants declared 2 to be **non-Standard**; 15 per cent of informants pointed out that *her family are* in 1 was ungrammatical, declaring that *her family is* should be the correct Standard form.

The responses are interesting in so far as judgements of Standard English are closely connected with judgements of formality. Of the three sentences, 3 is the most formal, while 2, still an example of Standard English, is the most informal. Sentence 2 is not ungrammatical, but it contains a markedly colloquial item – *bust* – which is more likely to be used in **contexts** of informal, **spoken** English. It is also interesting to note that most educated users of English remain uncertain as to the Standardness of *family are/is*, for in a separately administered test with the same group of informants, 52 per cent declared the sentence to be grammatically correct, while 37 per cent declared it to be incorrect (11 per cent remaining undecided or uncertain). (Some **grammars** draw a distinction between *the family are* (plural), as signifying reference to the family as a collective body of individuals, and *the family is* (singular), as signifying reference to the family as a sociological unit – in, for example, the sentence 'The family is under threat in modern Britain'.)

It is revealing that Standard English is broadly equated with what is grammatically correct even though considerable uncertainty obtains as to what constitutes such correctness. Attitudes to vocabulary, especially to the perceived formality of **lexical** items, also plays a part in determining judgements of Standardness.

1.2 Language and language change: historical perspectives

This brief section examines Standard English from a historical perspective.

ACTIVITY

Read the following brief account of the history of the development of Standard English in Britain. The account is based on Milroy and Milroy (1991) and Leith (1983) – two sources which can be consulted for further, more detailed explanation. After reading the account, give two advantages and two disadvantages which result from such a process of Standardization.

1b

In Britain during the period from the eleventh century (the time of the French invasion) to the fourteenth century, English was not widely used for official purposes. The dominant languages were Norman French and Latin (the language of the Church). English existed mainly in spoken forms, within which there were considerable **dialect** *variations between different parts of the country. The first major literary work in English, Chaucer's <u>Canterbury Tales</u>, was published at the end of the fourteenth century and was written in Chaucer's own dialect, that of the East Midlands. The advent of printing-presses, established by William Caxton at Westminster in 1476, gave great impetus to written English. However, as more and more official documents were produced, and as most of those educated to write studied at the universities of Oxford and Cambridge, the dialect of London and the eastern and Midlands* *regions of the country was, not unsurprisingly, adopted as the language of national written communication. As a result, other dialectal varieties of British English failed to acquire the same status. The growth of the East Midlands dialect as a national language led to its increasing codification and prescription, particularly in the seventeenth and eighteenth centuries, in grammar books and usage manuals. The dialect of one part of the country thus became the national, standard written language for the whole country.*

(Author's data)

The disadvantages of the establishment of a standard national language are as follows:
—although the selection of the East Midlands dialect as the standard, national **written language** is no more than a geographical and historical accident, such historical explanations do nothing to enhance the status of those dialects which have as a result become 'non-Standard' and thus increasingly downgraded and stigmatized. It appears as if the Standard dialect is inherently superior, particularly because it is unambiguously associated with writing and with written literacy;
—without such a historical perspective, which few people actually possess, dialects of English can easily be seen negatively as 'non-Standard' – as corruptions or 'incorrect' versions of the Standard 'correct' version. Many people speak other dialects as the standard but can come to be judged as linguistically inferior as a result. (For a fuller account see Giles and Powesland, 1975.)

One of the main advantages of the development of a standard language is that the particular dialect concerned becomes more fully elaborated so that it can serve a wide variety of purposes. In particular, it develops an extensive range of vocabulary and a variety of structures which can be deployed for purposes of public, formal and written communication. The standard dialect

4

grows organically as the standard language for national (and eventually international) communication, and serves as a basic variety which is, and can therefore be taught as being, comprehensible to all.

Consider the following extracts carefully. Each has been taken from books that have been written about the English language, ranging in date from the 1830s to the 1990s. Try to assemble them into some kind of rough chronological order, and identify specifically the particular views they present of Standard English.

1c

The great difficulty of teachers in Elementary Schools in many districts is that they have to fight against the powerful influences of evil habits of speech contracted in home and street. The teachers' struggle is thus not with ignorance but with a perverted power. That makes their work the harder, but it also makes their zeal the fiercer. A child with home advantages hears English used well, and grows up to use it well himself. He speaks grammatically, he acquires a wide vocabulary, he collects ideas.

1d

At the centre of the new orthodoxy is its devaluation of Standard English. From this derives its opponents' hostility to grammatical prescription: because they do not believe that Standard English is superior to dialect, they do not believe that its grammar should be prescribed to children (a position they try to support by mistakenly insisting that grammar cannot ever prescribe); because they cannot accept that Standard English is superior to dialect, they insist that the language schoolchildren use can be judged only by its 'appropriateness'.

1e

The common standard dialect is that in which all marks of a particular place of birth and residence are lost and nothing appears to indicate any other habits of intercourse than with the well-bred and well-informed, wherever they may be found . . . It may be that a person cannot altogether reach this standard; but if he reach it very nearly, all the object of a complete uniformity may be gained. A person needs not blush because he cannot help betraying that he is a Scotchman or an Irishman; but it may nevertheless be an object of ambition to prove that his circle of intercourse has extended much beyond his native place.

1f

No language is, or ever has been, in the strict sense of the word, 'pure'. All languages are continually borrowing and lending – adopting words from foreign sources, and contributing from their own store to that of others.

1g

The overthrow of grammar coincided with the acceptance of the equivalent of creative writing in social behaviour. As nice points of grammar were mockingly dismissed as pedantic and irrelevant, so was punctiliousness in such matters as honesty, responsibility, property, gratitude, apology and so on.

1h

Standard English is, in essentials, the best of the English dialects, and therefore – though foreign languages may excel it in this or that quality – one of the most subtle and most beautiful of all expressions of the human spirit.

1i

If pupils do not have access to Standard English then many important opportunities are closed to them, in cultural activities, in further and higher education, and in industry, commerce and the professions. Those educationalists who deny children these oppor-

tunities are confining them to the ghetto, to a restricted discourse which will close to them access not only to the professions but also to leadership in national politics. In our democracy, Standard English confers power on its users, power to explain political issues and to persuade on a national and international stage. This right should not be denied to any child.

1j
Every time the question of the language surfaces, in one way or another, it means that a series of other problems are coming to the fore: the formation and enlargement of the governing class, the need to establish more intimate and secure relationships between the governing groups and the national–popular mass, in other words to reorganize the cultural hegemony.

Text **1c**: Henry Newbolt (1921) *The Teaching of English in England*. The Newbolt Report, originally published by HMSO in 1921, sees the process of education as a means of 'intervening with history'. This process is a way of restoring 'harmony and peace'. It regards English as the only possible basis for providing students with a national education, and argues that the different classes in England are divided by the distinctly recognizable ways in which they speak. The teaching of a particular form of the English language (in this case, Standard English) is seen as a possible way of creating a 'bond of union' between such divisions, thereby reinstating national pride.

Its emphasis, however, specifically views the majority as speaking an inferior language (*the evil habits of speech contracted in home and street*), and there is a general exhortation to present such people with 'civilized speech' (in this instance, Standard English). This is the model to which all children should aspire – a speech that is not 'disfigured with vulgarisms', and whose pronunciation is similarly exempt from regional influences.

There is, here, an attempt to create national unity by urging pupils to make use of a particular form of the language that is regarded as the one used by 'the cultured and the educated'; any other forms of the language are seen as vulgar and uneducated. It could be argued that such assertions are doubly destructive: what is intended to bring about unity and harmony simply reinforces inferiority and division.

Text **1d**: John Marenbon (1987) *English Our English – the new orthodoxy examined*. Published by the Centre for Policy Studies, this document represents the current thinking on education in the 1990s by right-wing politicians. Here, language is used to foster both social and cultural identity. There is a strong emphasis on the superiority of Standard English forms of the language; and a belief that concepts of 'appropriateness' in relationship to language use (matching suitability of expression to context) are the product of woolly-minded liberalism.

On the one hand, there seems to be a plea to return to Victorian values by means of reaffirming Standard English as a way of establishing a single and unified cultural and social identity, but there is also an acknowledgement that speakers very often switch codes of address, which conform to different rules and which follow different patterns of usage according to the particular context.

As with these and other claims, what is urged is a return to some kind of 'golden age', which, through its use of Standard English, could reflect a set of values that would embody an 'acceptable' society.

Text **1e**: B. H. Smart (1836) *Walker Remodelled – a new critical pronouncing dictionary*. Smart similarly offers ways of improving on what he regards as 'defects of utterance'. Likewise, he focuses on considering that 'dialect from which they all deviate'. In his terms, all other forms of the language need to be evaluated alongside this 'norm'. The *common standard dialect* is that which reflects 'good breeding' and intellectualism; Standard English is the language of the *well-bred and well-informed*; it is the kind of language to which the good English-language user should aspire.

The Standard form of English becomes a means of communicating that can avoid the difficulties and embarrassments associated with non-Standard usage. It is, however, interesting to note that Smart craves 'indulgence' to 'foreigners' for their lack of fully coming to terms with the Standard forms of the language, whilst berating regional users of English.

For Smart, the term *standard* relates to a level of excellence that is to be reached by the language producer. It is important to reach this level in order to gain social acceptance. Standard English, therefore, is seen as a form of language use from which all others (that is, non-Standard forms) deviate.

Text **1f**: G. F. Graham (1869) *A Book About Words*. Graham argues that languages are not free-standing or self-sufficient, and can never be seen as 'untainted' by historical connections with other languages. The argument here is that linguistic boundaries are amongst the most difficult both to identify and to fix.

Throughout the argument there is a recognizable conflict between a desire to retain the 'purity' of the language and an acknowledgement of the impossibility of changing naturally-developing rules and tendencies. All attempts to 'police' the language are seen as doomed to failure; and what counts as 'acceptable' or 'proper' English, at any one particular point in time, depends upon constantly changing and flexible ways of speaking and writing.

Text **1g**: John Rae (1982) *The Decline and Fall of English Grammar*. Rae is here referring to the so-called decline in teaching of traditional grammar in the English school system, and the ostensibly uninhibited 'freedom' of the creative writing movement. Such falling standards, Rae argues, inevitably lead to a decline in literacy. The blame for this decline is placed upon the abandonment of formal grammar teaching, and its subsequent replacement by creative writing teaching. However much the case is to the contrary, individual assertions predominate. Language and morality are also seen as interdependent: a decline in one leads to an inevitable decline in the other.

Text **1h**: R. W. Chapman (1932) *Oxford English*. Contrary to expectations, early modern British linguists were not neutral, scientific observers of aspects of language which were neither praised nor censured; many were involved in the relationship between the study of language and their own social and attitudinal concerns about English. Chapman, for example, sees Standard English as *the best of the English dialects* – almost among the finest of the languages in the world. Again, the emphasis is upon the nature of the language reflecting the essence of the *human spirit*. Standard English holds a predominance because of its prestige – its national and international reputation – but also because it has an essential, intrinsic 'worth'.

Text **1i**: Brian Cox (1991) *Cox on Cox – an English Curriculum for the 1990s*. Cox affirms the development of the ability to produce Standard English in both written and spoken forms as a *right* for every child. However, he does acknowledge that, in trying to achieve this objective, certain aspects of the nature of Standard English need to be clarified:

—Standard English should never be regarded as 'fixed' in its format. It constantly changes over time, like any other language, and teachers of English need to be sensitive to this change;

—teachers need to be aware that it has many variations (both in form and use); and that such variations are brought about according to the style, purpose and audience of the text. There is no one form of Standard English;

— Standard English must not be equated with 'good' English and non-Standard with 'bad'. Producers of Standard forms of the language are as capable of producing 'bad' English as non-Standard users;

— it is more problematic to develop a pupil's ability to produce spoken Standard English than it is to develop a pupil's competence in written Standard English. Because of home and peer-group pressure, teachers can have little hope of changing how pupils speak;

— a crucial requirement in the development of pupils' ability to produce a varied linguistic repertoire is to place them in situations where they can talk about, and reflect upon, the nature of language in use.

Text **1j**: Antonio Gramsci (1910) *Cultural Writings*. The creation and development of a 'national' language was very much the concern of nineteenth-century Italy, where, until the unification in 1861, most Italians made use of one of a large number of dialects. Gramsci, a political theorist and historical linguist, saw the need to create a common national language, but he also recognized the problems related to the social constructions of such forms.

Any form of the language, be it Standard English or another variety, has to develop within the society in which it is produced, and this by a continuing process of regulation and alteration, dependent on the different conditions of its use in changing circumstances. It is in no way fixed by individual producers, or by those who claim a particular cultural or moral allegiance.

1.3 Language in context

Any approach to the study of the role of Standard English needs to be seen in the context of actual language production – in relation to the function of specific uses of English in particular situations.

ACTIVITY

Read through the following extracts from a variety of different **texts** (both narrative and non-narrative), focusing in particular on the following aspects:
— identify the situation in which each of these texts was produced.
— specify any difficulties you encountered in understanding any of the texts.
— state which text you found easiest to understand, and why.

1k

USING DISKS

This section covers the use of disks:
● *different types of floppy disks*
● *how to format floppy disks*
● *how to write-protect, label and back up floppy disks*
● *looking after floppy disks*
● *backing up a hard disk*
● *looking after a hard disk.*
You can store computer programs and data on floppy disks (sometimes called diskettes) and/or hard disks. Floppy disks are inserted into the computer; hard disks are permanently fixed inside the computer and are sometimes called 'winchester' or 'fixed' disks.

Floppy disks
Floppy disks come in two physical sizes: 3.5" disks and 5.25" disks. Your computer uses 3.5" floppy disks.

All NB3000 computers have a floppy disk drive that accepts two types of 3.5" floppy disks:

- *1.44Mb disks, known as high-density disks. High-density disks can be recognized by the two square holes in the casing, and usually have 'HD' printed on the disk.*
- *720Kb disks, known as low-density (or double-density) disks. These have one square hole in the disk casing, and are often marked 'DD'. These disks do not hold as much data as high-density disks.*

Low-density 3.5" disks formatted using the /F:720 switch can be used on all RM computers that run MS-DOS (see page 55).

Identifying floppy disk drives
On an NB300, the floppy disk drive is referred to as drive A.

Preparing new floppy disks for use
New disks must be 'formatted' before you can use them to store data. Make sure that the disk you want to format is not write-protected, otherwise you will not be able to format it. Write-protected means that you can read data that is on the disk but you cannot change the data or write new data to the disk. (See 'Write-protecting floppy disks' below for instructions on write-protection.)

> *Caution: if you format a disk that already has information stored on it, all the information on the disk is deleted. You can attempt to recover this information using the UNFORMAT command.*

For instructions on using the FORMAT command to format disks, see Chapter 6.
(Research Machines plc, 1992)

1l

A GUESSING GAME STARTS

The guessing game has already started – who is staying and who will be shown the door at Sheffield Steelers?

Coach Alex Dampier is privately mulling over his thoughts on assembling a squad capable of fulfilling his ambitions and those of the biggest crowds in Premier history.

Much depends on a possible change in the status of reclassified players like Steelers' Tim Cranston.

Around 30 foreign-born players already in the UK could be classed as British under new rules being considered. That would open the floodgates to wealthier clubs like Sheffield, especially if wage ceilings are adjusted or scrapped.

Dampier will be influenced by the form of his core players on the Wembley stage if they get there.

The coach has already dropped a broad hint that Selmar Odelein's position is secure.

And I expect him to stand by his veteran defensive partner Chris Kelland, who has been a consistent performer throughout his first season at the Arena.

The 36-year-old may have the clock against him but his steadying influence is an important factor. The Canadian also has British status after years in the UK game.

Rumours that Les Millie may be on his way back to Scotland, where he has an offer of work, are groundless.

'I'll be staying here if they have me,' he said today.

Fans will also want to know whether favourites like captain Ron Shudra, most recent addition Ivan Matulik and dedicated pro Steve Nemeth will be retained.

Matulik says: 'I'll be going back to Canada in the summer and will be thinking about the future then.

'If I come back to this country then, of course, I would want to play for Steelers.'

Youngsters like Danny Boome and Scott Heaton also want to stay – but would probably want their contracts put on a sounder financial footing.

(Bob Westerdale, *Sheffield Star*, 15 March 1994)

1m

ERNEST HEMINGWAY'S TYPIST

It sounds like religious music. A friend of mine just came back from New York where he had Ernest Hemingway's typist do some typing for him.

He's such a successful writer, so he went and got the very best, which happens to be the woman who did Ernest Hemingway's typing. It's enough to take your breath away, to marble your lungs with silence.

Ernest Hemingway's typist!

She's every young writer's dream come true with the appearance of her hands which are like a harpsichord and the perfect intensity of her gaze and all to be followed by the profound sound of her typing.

He paid her fifteen dollars an hour. That's more money than a plumber or an electrician gets.

$120 a day! for a typist!

He said that she does everything for you. You just hand her the copy and like a miracle you have attractive, correct spelling and punctuation that is so beautiful that it brings tears to your eyes and paragraphs that look like Greek temples and she even finishes sentences for you.

She's Ernest Hemingway's,

She's Ernest Hemingway's typist.

(Brautigan 1971)

1n

ROBOT IS WINNER BY A NOSE

A revolutionary new computer that can sniff out the difference between cheap plonk and the finest wines, detect fake perfume and even tell a doctor what's wrong with you was unveiled yesterday.

And when the Daily Mirror put the electronic marvel through its paces it beat an expert winetaster by a nose.

The £10,000 machine, called The Nose, identified expensive wines within 30 seconds just by the smell – including some which had our expert baffled.

Nick Ryman Tubb, boss of the firm that jointly developed the computer, said: 'The Nose can tell a wine's pedigree by identifying the grape and vineyard just like a human connoisseur.'

But the British invented robot, which took four years to develop, is more than just a toy to put the connoisseurs out of business.

It could be used to create new perfumes – or detect whether you are wearing Chanel No 5 or some conman has sold you a fake.

One whiff from a food production line could tell makers if a cheese is mature or things are not up to standard.

And in the cola wars, manufacturers could program it to find out just how a rival's products are made.

The Nose could even save lives, analysing a patient's breath to detect illnesses – and is currently undergoing trials on lung cancer patients.

A spokesman for the Department of Trade and Industry, which is publicising the computer, said: 'It is really world class technology and here in Britain we are at the forefront.'

(Tanith Carey, *Daily Mirror*, 15 March 1994)

1o

THE STRUCTURE OF KNOWLEDGE

The central assumption of connectionist theories of learning is that knowledge is built upon the elements, pieces, or components of our experiences but that it consists of learned relations among them. Because these theories of learning are built from the bottom or most elementary levels of representation up, the easiest way to understand their logic may also be from the bottom up. For a moment, imagine that you are a baby.

Perhaps even in your first encounter with a rectangle, you see it as a whole. But inside, the wholeness of this new pattern is represented as an appropriately interrelated set of four line segments. The rectangle is created from your prior knowledge of its simpler parts by linking them in a new and particular interrelation with one another.

Having once been studied, the rectangle's perceptual support will now be different, for the interrelated assemblage of parts it aroused must now reside in your memory. On next encounter, it will be received by the entire, connected representation of its prior occurrence, and you will respond to it as a familiar whole. The more you encounter or study it, the stronger those interrelations will grow, the more familiar (better remembered) it will become as a whole, and the more quickly you will respond to it as such.

Still, no matter how many times you see this rectangle and no matter how well-integrated and holistically familiar it becomes, it will at core be comprised of the same set of interrelations among the same elementary line segments. When you encounter some different rectangle, it too must be perceived as an interrelated set of four line segments. And as you encounter another, and another, and another, you will eventually accrue a whole lot of rectangle memories that as a group substantially overlap. Each will share some aspects of its underlying representation with others, and each of those, in turn, may overlap with your first rectangle, with each other, or with still others. In this way, what will accrue is a family or distribution of rectangles, perceptually bound together by their common representational base. In perceiving rectangle, after rectangle, after rectangle, you will eventually come to perceive each as a member of a class.

In this oneness of the core representations of knowledge, lies only half the key to learning.
(Adams 1990)

A reader's reaction to different texts seems to be influenced by three main factors:

1. The reader's previous knowledge of the subject matter;
2. The reader's own motivation to make sense of what is being read;
3. The writer's anticipation of the needs of the expected audience.

Such factors need to be considered carefully when looking at the function of Standard English in a variety of different contexts.

Text **1k** is taken from the *User Guide to the NB300 Research Machine*. Its intended readers, therefore, may have no previous knowledge of the subject, but, if they are keen to learn how to operate computers, they are likely to have the motivation to make, or seek, meaning from the text. The writer establishes the reader as a 'willing novice' and, in some instances, attempts to present information in an accessible way. For instance, the reader is personally addressed (*You can store*; *the disk you want to format*; *you can read*). There is also some attempt to explain specific items of information (*sometimes called diskettes*; *known as high-density/low-density disks*; *Write-protected means that you can read data that is on the disk but you cannot change the data*). There are also references to further support in alternative sections (*For instructions on using the FORMAT command to format disks, see Chapter 6*). However, the language itself presents problems from its very technical nature; assumptions are made, for instance, in terms of understanding vocabulary items such as *floppy disks, computer programs, winchester/fixed disks, formatted*.

Readers who are more or less 'computer literate' will probably have found least difficulty with this text, but some readers may have refused to engage with the text when its subject matter was first revealed. This may have been on principle, but it may also have been based on previous, unsuccessful experiences of trying to understand computer information. Certainly, the grammatical and lexical items present some 'distancing' difficulties:

—the use of passives (*are inserted, is referred to*)

—assumptions of 'meaning' (*write-protect, formatted*).

For motivated readers, perhaps, further reading of the section of the User Guide from which this extract is taken allows them to ignore the technicalities presented here and simply to follow a set of instructions. Experienced readers of this kind of material will recognize that they do not necessarily need to understand such detailed information as is found in this extract in order to be able to operate the computer.

Text **1l** is a report of an ice-hockey team's progress, taken from the sports pages of a regional newspaper in England. Its intended readers may have an interest in a wide range of sport and may have read coverage of this particular type of sporting activity. Without such referential knowledge, however, the report is largely meaningless since the writer has made no concessions to a more general audience: ice hockey is never mentioned, but there are references to similar 'competitive' games – *Coach, squad, players, clubs, defensive, Fans*. Interestingly, the vocabulary and **syntax** is often framed in informal/casual terms: *guessing game, shown the door, mulling over, open the floodgates, scrapped, stand by*. In fact, much of the report is constructed on an informal, speech-oriented basis: *And I expect him*; *who will be shown the door at Sheffield Steelers?*, *the 36-year-old may have the clock against him*. Because of such informality, the text should prove easy to read, even if it is difficult to identify the specific sport!

Text **1m** appears in one of a series of 'stories' in Richard Brautigan's *Revenge of the Lawn* (1962–70). As a 'story' it presents some interesting features; many of its features reflect more aspects of a personal, spoken and anecdotal style of delivery, emphasizing the features of casual letter-writing such as:

—exclamations: *Ernest Hemingway's typist!*;

—personalizations: *You just hand her the copy*;

—clichéd utterances: *It's enough to take your breath away*.

On the other hand, there is also evidence of more Standard and 'crafted' constructions of language use: *to marble your lungs with silence*; *She's Ernest Hemingway's, She's Ernest Hemingway's typist*.

Text **1n** is taken from a recent issue of a popular tabloid newspaper, the *Daily Mirror*. Here, the relationship between writer and reader is assumed to be fairly casual and informal. Vocabulary items consist of many idiomatic expressions: *sniff out*, *cheap plonk*, *put ... through its paces*, *whiff*. Similarly, syntactic devices reflect a 'speech-driven' model of communication – *And when ...*; *And in the cola wars ...* – as does paragraphing by sentence. Easy understanding of this text comes from its reliance on using spoken forms of English 'written down', and from its assumptions of intertextual knowledge (*winner by a nose*).

Text **1o** is an extract from an academic textbook specifically aimed at teachers in primary education. Taken from Marilyn Jager Adams's book *Beginning to Read* (1990), its intended reader is the language specialist who is attempting to find out more about issues to do with the teaching of early reading. Therefore, a reader (and, in particular, a primary-school teacher with a specific interest in English teaching) will have the motivation to make sense of it, especially if they are prepared to read it with careful concentration (even rereading the text and making 'mental' or 'physical' notes).

On the one hand, certain knowledge is assumed on the part of the reader: *connectionist theories of learning*, *built from the bottom*, *interrelated assemblage*, *connected representation*. On the other hand, the writer is trying to explain her ideas clearly by elaborating, metaphorically, on her use of terminology: *Perhaps even in your first encounter with a rectangle*. Explanation comes from creating parallel instances (the rectangle) and identifying the reader personally (*your memory*, *you encounter*, *you will respond*). The passage can stand on its own, although it is also, obviously, part of an ongoing text – 'The Structure of Knowledge' being a subsection of a particular chapter of the book, 'The Nature of Learning'.

This text perhaps highlights another factor which influences our reading: how far we share the writer's assumptions or ideology. In this case, we may be drawn in, or alienated from, such a text if we do, or do not, share its author's beliefs – in this case, specific attitudes to the way in which children should learn to read.

Generally speaking, with this text, the key to reading for understanding lies in the motivation of the reader to make meaning, rather than relying on referential knowledge or finding alternative information or instructions to read.

When considering the nature of Standard English (both spoken and written), attention needs to be paid to its variability. For English to retain its vitality and creativity, it has to be seen in the context of its continuing adaptability to use in a wide variety of differing situations (both formal and informal). 'It is generally accepted that communities ... should be granted rights of ownership and allowed to fashion the language of their needs' (Widdowson 1993: 7). It is in the spirit of this assertion that the exploration in the following chapters, of the nature of spoken and written Standard English, is made.

SUMMARY

- Attitudes to Standard English seem to be closely connected to judgements on the formality of utterances.
- Standard English is usually equated with what is thought to be grammatically correct, although there is considerable uncertainty as to what constitutes such correctness.
- It is useful to view the development of Standard English from a historical perspective.

- Standard English needs to be studied in the context of language in use, and as textual data, not as isolated grammatical or lexical features.

2 Standard English and standards of English

Now hear this. You are mountain people. You hear me? Your
language is dead. It is forbidden. It is not permitted to speak
your mountain language in this place. You cannot speak your
language to your men. It is not permitted. Do you understand?
You may not speak it. It is outlawed. You may only speak the
language of the capital. That is the only language permitted in
this place. You will be badly punished if you attempt to speak
your mountain language in this place. This is a military decree. It
is the law. Your language is forbidden. It is dead. No one is
allowed to speak your language. Your language no longer exists.

Harold Pinter, *Mountain Language*

Our view of Standard English, and its definition, has always
been determined by our own attitudes and prejudices. Standard
English requires careful and systematic investigation as there is
a great deal of confusion and misunderstanding about its nature
and influences. Once again in England, the teaching of Standard
English has become a major issue in the sphere of language in
education. Any investigation, therefore, of its features and influences needs to consider the origins of our feelings and opinions
about it.

An initial concern is the variety of interpretations people
give to the word 'standard'. Over the years it has been linked
with several meanings – 'correct', 'accurate', 'good', 'proper' –
each sense presenting a slightly different perspective, but most

conveying a feeling of the 'superiority' of Standard English over other Englishes.

2.1 What is meant by Standard?

A suitable starting point to investigate the nature of Standard English and its uses is to explore the variety of different meanings and connotations the word 'standard' can have.

ACTIVITY

What is meant by the term standard?

This activity is designed to explore the potential multiplicity of meanings and associations that the word 'standard' can have in a variety of spoken and written contexts. Think of as many different uses of the word 'standard' as you can. If possible, it might be useful to work with a partner. Make a list of those meanings, preferably placing their use in a particular context; for example, 'A "standard" lamp is a central feature of many living rooms, where "standard" means "free-standing".'

The point of this activity is to draw attention to the wide variation of meanings the word 'standard' can have in everyday use, and how some of these meanings might well influence our interpretation of the term 'Standard English'.

A useful source of comparison is Raymond Williams's *Keywords* (1976), where he lists several examples of the use of the word 'standard', which reveal a variety of different meanings in everyday use:

— royal standard/standard-bearer (meaning 'a distinctive flag or symbol of authority');

— gold standard (meaning 'a basic unit of comparison');

— <u>standard</u> foot (meaning 'an authorized unit of measurement');
— <u>standard</u> size (meaning 'the usual' or 'the accepted');
— <u>standard</u> model (meaning 'basic' or 'minimum specification');
— <u>standard</u> work (meaning 'that of an accepted authority' – as in 'the standard work on the French Revolution');
— maintaining <u>standards</u> (meaning 'attaining a particular level in some hierarchy where no precise measurement is possible');
— moral <u>standards</u> (meaning 'behaviour that is acceptable within a certain group or society');
— <u>standardization</u> (meaning 'the process of making everything conform to the same basic requirements'; its meaning is usually pejorative).

This list is not intended to be definitive in any way, but an analysis of the shifts in the meaning of the term 'standard' should show that not one but several of its meanings might well be involved in people's complex interpretations of 'Standard' English (for example, 'distinctive', 'correct', 'basic', 'authorized', 'usual', 'accepted', 'superior', 'measurable', and so on).

The activity, at the very least, should reveal your own attitudes to the term, as well as the similarities or differences in the attitudes of others.

ACTIVITY

What is meant by the term <u>correct</u>?

This activity is designed to complement the preceding one by specifically focusing on the contrasts in meaning of the words 'correct' and 'standard'. Again, it might be useful to work with a partner.

Consider the following sentences, identifying the 'errors', if possible. Try and identify which sentences are correct and which are 'Standard' and determine whether there is any distinction between the two terms. In your investigation it would be helpful to place the use of these sentences in specific spoken or written contexts (to discover, for instance, whether your understanding of a 'correct' or 'incorrect' form, or a 'Standard' or 'non-Standard' form, is influenced by its occurrence in speech or in writing, or by its occurrence in different social contexts, both public and popular).

2a
1. *Everyone has their off-days.*
2. *He only had one chapter to finish.*
3. *He is older than me.*
4. *She did it quick.*
5. *It was impossible to even think of it.*
6. *I never did nothing.*
7. *We was going to do it later.*
(Author's data)

1. It is commonly accepted that pronouns following such words as *everyone*, *anyone* and *no one* take a singular form – in this case *his/her*. Yet the move away from gender distinction has led to the plural form *their* being frequently used, particularly in speech.
2. The position that is usually chosen for the adverb *only* is closest to the item it immediately qualifies – in this case *He had only one chapter to finish*. But, finally, the choice must rest on the meaning intended. Meaning may be clarified further in speech by intonation; in writing, the author has to decide whether a change of order affects intention.
3. The influence of Latin grammar in English causes some traditional linguists to assert that *me* is here in the <u>accusative</u> case. As they interpret the 'full' sentence to read *He is older than I (am old)*, they argue that *I* in the <u>nominative</u> case should be the form used.

4. Several adverbs are formed by adding -ly to the adjective, but this ending, in many instances, appears to be optional: *cheap/cheaply*, *fair/fairly*. The correctness of this sentence depends on whether you think that *quick/quickly* falls into the same category and that -ly is, therefore, an optional choice.
5. Some grammarians would condemn the use of the split infinitive *to even think* (placing a word or words between *to* and the verb), but its use dates back to the thirteenth century. Many take the line, 'Don't use a split infinitive unless you have a good reason for doing so'!
6. An example of multiple negation – a form found in some non-Standard forms of English. It is often condemned (erroneously) on grounds of logic: two negatives make a positive.
7. *We was going* is a non-Standard grammatical form of English – the Standard form being *were*.

As we saw in the opening chapter, investigating attitudes to each of these sentences in a wide variety of different social contexts (both spoken and written) should raise some, if not all, of the following issues:
— how important it is to consider the role of 'context' when discussing correctness or appropriateness;
— the need to relate the acceptance of certain linguistic forms to their appearance in speech or in writing, or in both;
— how far the grammatical description of the Latin language should be allowed to influence and determine English use;
— the variety of connotations the word 'standard' might have when using the term 'Standard English';
— the notion that language forms are never static and that attitudes to acceptability and correctness change over time.

The two complementary activities above are designed to highlight some of the problems of identifying and describing Standard English for teachers. As Stubbs (1988) states: 'A major role for linguistics is the steady unpicking of unreflecting beliefs and myths about language, especially where such beliefs affect the lives of all children in schools' (page 3). It is very important to try and disentangle some of the 'beliefs' and 'myths' that Stubbs refers to, in an attempt[2] to define Standard English clearly and accurately. However, McCabe (1990) introduces a further complication:

The theoretical problem is in defining the standard language which lies at the core of the [Cox] Report. The Report is unequivocal on the social need to master the written standard. To be unable to write Standard English or to use its spoken forms in appropriate public contexts is to be disenfranchised, to be deprived of true citizenship ... Where it is appropriate to use the standard, you use it but there are many uses where other forms, or other languages, are as appropriate ... It is astonishing to reflect that no linguistic theory has even begun to pose the question of the permissible range of variation within a standard although it is obvious even from the history of English that the range is not fixed. (page 11)

In the light of recent recommendations in England that Standard English be taught in schools and that teachers develop a consistent policy adapting such recommendations to their own particular circumstances, there is clearly no agreement as to what exactly Standard English is. Stubbs (1988) suggests that it is almost a circular argument: Standard English is the language used in education – education must use Standard English. McCabe (1990) raises the additional problem of variation and flexibility within the 'standard', both in and across time.

These points are not just matters of linguistic debate; they affect educational and social practice in quite radical ways. The debate on attitudes to, and the teaching of, Standard English in England over the past decade has, unfortunately, all too often centred on a very narrow and prejudiced view of what it actually is. Consider some of the following comments:

We've allowed so many standards to slip. Teachers weren't bothering to teach kids to spell and punctuate properly. If you allow standards to slip to the stage where good English is no better than bad English, where people turn up filthy at school. All those things cause people to have no standards at all, and once you lose standards then there's no imperative to stay out of crime. (Norman Tebbit, BBC Radio 4, 1985)

A better approach to English teaching in schools would reject every tenet of the new orthodoxy ... The teacher would not hesitate to prescribe to the children on matters of grammatical correctness. He [*sic*] would recognize the superiority of Standard English and see it as his task to make his pupils write it well and thereby gain the ability to speak it fluently. (John Marenbon, *English Our English*, 1987)

If we want people to write good English and write plays for the future, it cannot be done with the present system, and all the nonsense academics come up with. It is a fundamental problem. We must educate for character. This matters a great deal. The whole way schools are operating is not right. I do not believe English is being taught properly. You cannot educate people properly unless you do it on a basic framework and drilling system. (Prince Charles, 28 June 1989)

Language is about communication. Incorrect language hampers that process. Children who cannot write correct English lose out in life to those who can. (Melanie Phillips, *Guardian*, 9 October 1992)

Such statements on Standard English and attitudes to English and English teaching in general are based upon views of English that are deeply rooted in the prejudices and opinions of people who are committed to an erroneously simplistic model of what the English language is:
— the English that we speak and write is somehow related to our standards of behaviour;
— Standard English is the correct form of the English language and, by this definition, is superior to all other forms of English;
— writing 'correct' English will help people to speak more effectively;

— defining Standard English is simply a matter of identifying what is 'right' and what is 'wrong'.

Such views are clearly not based on aspects of the English language that linguists and teachers would identify:

— the differences between spoken and written English;
— the notion that 'correctness' is relative;
— the relationship between language use and language context;
— the uses of English as an international language;
— the need to clarify 'Standard' in terms of both grammar and vocabulary;
— the importance of acknowledging that language changes over time.

Language is, indeed, a complex social phenomenon. It would be considerably easier for all of us if we could define Standard English simply as 'x' or 'y'. But neither language, nor indeed life, is that simple.

2.2 Variations and Standard English

If Standard English is not so simple, how complex is it really? And how 'describable' is it realistically in terms of how it is used nationally and internationally? It is perhaps easier, initially, to consider what Standard English is diagrammatically:

ENGLISH AND ENGLISHES

The first distinction to be made is between what we might artificially label English English and the English spoken and written in other parts of the English-speaking world. There are obvious differences in vocabulary: for example, American English has 'sidewalk' where English English has 'pavement'; Scottish English has 'kirk' where English English has 'church'. The same applies to other Englishes, both national and international.

ENGLISH AND ENGLISHES

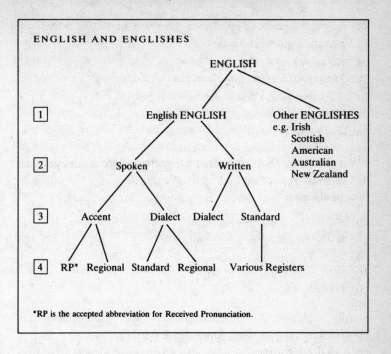

ENGLISH

1   English ENGLISH   Other ENGLISHES
                                    e.g. Irish
                                       Scottish
2   Spoken   Written   American
                                       Australian
                                       New Zealand
3   Accent   Dialect   Dialect   Standard

4   RP*   Regional   Standard   Regional   Various Registers

*RP is the accepted abbreviation for Received Pronunciation.

Differences in grammar, however, are not so immediately recognized. Perera (1987), in an extremely useful pamphlet, points out that standard <u>Scottish</u> English has a form 'These shoes need mended', where the Standard <u>English</u> English is 'These shoes need mending'. She also cites the use of 'gotten' in <u>American</u> English, showing, in fact, that the usage is consistent and has its own logic; in other words, the usage follows grammatical rules, although these rules are not those of <u>English</u> English.

ACTIVITY

Try putting these sentences into Standard American English, by using 'gotten' where necessary.

2b

1a. *I've got a new car recently.*
2a. *We've got off at the wrong stop.*
3a. *They'd got into trouble.*
4a. *She got very wet last night.*
5a. *He's got blue eyes.*

(Author's data)

We are aware that Americans use <u>gotten</u> where we use <u>got</u>, but not perhaps of the precise linguistic contexts where the different form will occur:

1b. *I've gotten a new car recently.*
2b. *We've gotten off at the wrong stop.*
3b. *They'd gotten into trouble.*
4b. *She got very wet last night.*
5b. *He's got blue eyes.*

Simply replacing all instances of <u>got</u> with <u>gotten</u> does not produce correct Standard American English because (i) <u>gotten</u> is only used after a part of <u>have</u> and so does not appear in **4**; and (ii) it is not used when <u>got</u> means 'have' or 'possess', as in **5**. Perera points out that, because she is not a native speaker of American English, she would have to check a grammar book (such as Trudgill and Hannah 1982) for these examples: her own ear does not tell her whether they are right or not (Perera 1987: 14).

Similar instances could be offered for other Englishes. The point to be made is that raising an awareness of the 'family' of languages we have come to know as English should also make us aware that there is a wide variety of 'Standard' forms; there is not one, universal variety that can be called 'the standard'. The point on an international level is identical to the one that McCabe (1990) makes on a national level: there is a range of variation within a standard.

At the next level of the diagram, we need to make a distinction between spoken and written forms of <u>English</u> English. The same distinction can, of course, be made for all the other Englishes, but from now on it will simplify matters if we concentrate on <u>English</u> English and refer to it simply as English.

Written English is relatively unchanging and standardized. For many students, learning to write also involves learning Standard English, since their habitual and natural way of speaking may well be in dialect. It is important to recognize that learning to write Standard English is a long and gradual process in which differentiating between spoken and written forms of that English is crucial. This needs to begin early and to be a consistent aspect of the teaching of writing. Also, how we draw attention to these differences and the language we use to do so are crucially important. This process needs to be seen as one of extending a student's language repertoire, while at the same time not denigrating the non-Standard dialects spoken by many. We should not, however, expect to achieve it overnight.

Although written English is standardized in many respects, there are, as has been noted already, many varieties of written English, and each possesses its own preferred vocabulary and grammatical choices. Examples include scientific, legal and medical English. Legal usage in all English-speaking communities tends to be fairly formal and grammatically quite complex. Sometimes archaic expressions are introduced, such as 'hereinafter', 'aforesaid' and 'thereto'. Similarly, scientific English has a complex style, related to its need to adopt an objective stance and convey details with great accuracy. Scientific English is 'characterized by:

— qualifying expressions such as "at least", "may", "probably", "under such conditions", "usually".
— parenthetical asides, intended to modify, support or otherwise affect statements: "according to the data", "apparently", "as far as we can tell at this stage".

— passive constructions serving to minimize or remove personality: "It was found that", "The data were analysed", "When completed", "the experiment was discussed".'
(McArthur 1992: 8)

Such varieties of English are identified by characteristic vocabulary and grammatical choices, although some make more obvious use of one rather than the other. Grammatical choices are, perhaps, most obvious in legal English. The complexity of the clause structure and the predominance of clauses of condition and consequence mark it as a distinct type of Standard Written English, and one which most of us who are not in the legal profession find difficult to read. In other varieties of Standard Written English, it is more commonly found that the subject-specific vocabulary is distinctive – in medical or religious English, for example. This does not, of course, invalidate the notion of Standard English, but it does reinforce the point that a definition of Standard English cannot be simple or clear-cut.

It is also legitimate to use dialect in written English for particular purposes. The most obvious is in dialogue (in a work of fiction or in a play script). Another is the conscious use of dialect to create a sense of regional identity. There are a few poets who write in dialect, and some writers have produced 'translations' of well-known texts (such as parts of the Bible) in dialect, usually for humorous effect.

However, although Standard Written English does not lend itself to a clear-cut classification, Standard Spoken English is even more difficult to categorize. The first major distinction that must be made is between <u>accent</u> and <u>dialect</u>. **Accent** refers to the sounds produced by speakers who come from a particular region or belong to a specific social class. For example, the way the 'a' sound is produced in such words as 'bath' and 'grass' will distinguish speakers from the North and South of England; this is an aspect of accent. Dialect refers to the particular features of grammar and vocabulary employed by the language user.

It is possible to speak Standard English in a range of accents. An utterance such as 'I was waiting until five for the bus' is Standard Spoken English, no matter how it is pronounced – whether the 'g' is sounded or not, and whatever the quality given to vowels such as those in 'I', 'until' and 'bus'. In dialect, however, the utterance might be changed to 'I were waiting while five for bus'. In this, both the vocabulary and the grammatical forms are changed. 'While' is a widely used regional dialect word for 'until' in the North of England, particularly in Yorkshire. It is not, of course, appropriate in Standard English, where 'until' is the preferred form. The grammatical form 'I were' is also a widely found dialect usage. In fact, the verb 'to be' in English is an interesting aspect of the Standard/dialect discussion. In Standard English, the forms are, in fact, irregular: I was, you were, s/he was, we were, they were. However, in various dialects we sometimes find a greater regularity: I were, you were, s/he were, we were, they were. In others, there is more irregularity: 'I been', 'we was', and so on.

Compare the following Standard and dialect versions of the personal pronoun system:

Standard English	Dialect
myself	myself
yourself	yourself
himself	hisself
herself	herself
ourselves	ourselves
themselves	theirselves

Sometimes dialect forms seem more logical, and students need to be able to distinguish between dialect forms and Standard forms, both of which are sometimes logical and sometimes illogical.

It is, of course, common to find regional dialect forms associated with regional accents. It would seem important to argue, in this respect, that students should not be discouraged from using their own accent, so long as this does not impair comprehension. However, in some situations, it is the case that a 'broad' regional accent can inhibit comprehension more than the use of vocabulary or grammatical dialect forms.

The use of Standard Spoken English (which, in effect, means not using regional dialect forms) is something that, like Standard Written English, has to be learned over a period of time and, in essence, requires students to feel motivated by seeing the need for more formal uses of language in particular contexts. As will be discussed later, drama and role-play activities can be helpful as one means of creating contexts in which Standard Spoken English is seen as necessary.

The discussion of Standard English and its particular attributes leads us to draw the following conclusions:
—in spite of recent press, media and government assertion, Standard English is not a term capable of being provided with an easy, clear-cut definition;
—it is, however, a term used frequently by some people as if they know precisely what it refers to;
—for many, it is always associated with the ideal of the language as produced by the 'good' or 'educated' users of English;
—it must not be regarded as a 'monolith' with more or less strict rules and conventions; instead, it can be seen to consist of overlapping varieties;
—it is regarded by many as a variety of English that has a considerable prestige;
—it is generally regarded as the variety of English most accepted and understood within an English-speaking country – more or less free of regional and class associations;

— it relates specifically to the grammatical and vocabulary forms of the language, and does not concern itself with questions of pronunciation (that is, accent);

— it is, in some senses, easier to define what is meant by Standard Written English than Standard Spoken English;

— it is also easier to identify and define Standard forms of grammar than Standard forms of vocabulary;

— standard forms are most clearly identified in print;

— there is a great danger in seeing the term 'Standard English' as being inevitably associated with 'standards of English'. It should never be seen to be, by its own nature, superior to any other dialectal form of the language. Many texts (both spoken and written) can be identified as using Standard forms of the language but can, nevertheless, be completely incomprehensible;

— it is also inappropriate to argue that there is a single, broadly recognizable international standard for English. Just as there are many different kinds of Standard English within Britain, there are many different kinds of international Standard English.

2.3   Standard and non-Standard English

ACTIVITY

The purpose of this activity is to explore some of the differences between Standard and non-Standard English (both written and spoken), and to consider some of the problems that such a polarity reveals.

Read through the four extracts featured below and, with a partner if possible, consider the texts in the light of these questions:

— is the text Standard English?

— what features mark it as either Standard or non-Standard?
— does it communicate readily and/or appropriately?

Text **2c** is an extract from *Sons and Lovers* by D. H. Lawrence. Text **2d** is the beginning of a long discussion of 'Postscript' by Louis MacNeice; those taking part are four first-year undergraduate students. Text **2e** is an extract from a legal document written over seventy years ago. Text **2f** is part of an article in the Media *Guardian*.

2c

She got ready and went by the first train to Derby, where she saw her son and the sergeant. It was, however, no good.

When Morel was having his dinner in the evening, she said suddenly:

'I've had to go to Derby today.'

The miner turned up his eyes, showing the whites in his black face.

'Has ter, lass. What took thee there?'

'That Arthur!'

'Oh – an' what's agate now?'

'He's only enlisted.'

Morel put down his knife and leaned back in his chair.

'Nay,' he said, 'that he niver 'as!'

'And is going down to Aldershot tomorrow.'

'Well!' exclaimed the miner. 'That's a winder.' He considered it a moment, said 'H'm!' and proceeded with his dinner. Suddenly his face contracted with wrath. 'I hope he may never set foot i' my house again,' he said.

'The idea!' cried Mrs Morel. 'Saying such a thing!'

'I do,' repeated Morel. 'A fool as runs away for a soldier, let 'im look after 'issen; I s'll do no more for 'im.'

'A fat sight you have done as it is,' she said.

And Morel was almost ashamed to go to his public-house that evening.

(D. H. Lawrence, *Sons and Lovers*)

This extract illustrates the distinction between the use of dialogue in a written context, where dialect is perfectly acceptable, and the accompanying narrative of a novel or short story, where, in many cases, it is not. Thus, Lawrence uses dialect forms in speech, such as *Has ter*, *lass*, *niver* and *'issen*, but in the narrative itself he maintains Standard English usage. Also, there is a more subtle distinction made between the dialect of Morel (local and working class) and the speech of Mrs Morel, which is represented in more Standard forms to indicate her social aspirations:

Mrs Morel: *I've had to go to Derby today.*
Morel: *Has ter, lass. What took thee there?*

There are, of course, no agreed conventions for writing down dialect forms. When Lawrence writes *Has ter*, he is attempting to create in our minds the sounds of Morel's accent as well as indicating the vocabulary and grammar of the Nottinghamshire dialect. He could as well have written *As't*. There are no rules for writing dialect down, except the general ones of suggestiveness and intelligibility.

2d

D: *Now we'll start at the beginning which is ... er ... that f-f-first two lines which is probably the most obvious well I think so anyway ... er ... mm when he says we were children words were coloured ... er ... and then in brackets ... er ... just as an aside sort of thing harlot and murder were dark purple why is harlot and especially murder dark purple(?) is that any reference to blood(?) (several voices) ... I think blood's not purple is it(?)*
(laughter)
C: *Jeremy's is*
J: *mine is*
D: *thought it was red*
S: *mixture of blue blood and ordinary blood*

D: I would say . . . well . . . purple's s'posed to be royal anyway

C & S: yeh . . . mm

C: but that might it of course the fact that . . . yeh . . . that . . .
mm

J: I was saving myself for that one

(laughter)

S: that they were idealized

C: no(.) that yeh . . . that they were . . . no . . . I wonder if it's
purple royal it wasn't in contact with him it was something
royal(.) you know how royal things are out of contact with
ordinary people . . . mm

S: yeh but

D: yeh

C: there were things that he only heard about from a distance(.)
he wasn't actually tainted by things like harlot

J: yeh but why throw it in as an aside sort of thing in brackets

C: yeh

J: I think it's more or less to – to . . . say you know . . . er . . . the
. . . sort of colour scheme for various feelings.

(Author's data)

Three of the four students taking part in this discussion have accents that, while not particularly prominent, nevertheless mark them as from the North of England. The fourth is from the Midlands. These characteristics are not, of course, apparent in the transcript – a point which emphasizes that accent is a matter of the choices made from a range of sounds that are possible in English. This is a different issue to the use of Standard and non-Standard English dialects, in which grammar and vocabulary choice are the main variables.

As is always the case when looking at transcripts of speech, we have, first and foremost, to come to terms with the actual 'texture' of the conversation – the interruptions, the unfinished statements, the hesitations and the reformulations. It appears untidy and quite unlike writing; but that does not, in itself, make it non-Standard English. These features are particularly evident in exploratory discussion of this nature. In fact, in this particular text there are no examples of non-Standard grammar or vocabulary.

2e

ALL THAT pce of land contg 812 supfl sq yds or thrabts frontg to King Egbert Road leadg out of Totley Brook Road in the Psh of Dore in the Coy of Derby and delnd and cold pink and green on the plan drawn on abstg psnts

AND ALSO ALL THOSE two messes of dwghses and out-bldgs then recently ered on the sd pce of land

TOGR with a right of foot horse and carre way at all times and for all ppses over along and across King Egbert Road afsd and a right of drainage through the sewers and drains thrunder
(Deed of sale)

This (it must be admitted) is a bit of a rarity! It is probably difficult to decode without some effort on the part of the reader and without some prior acquaintance with the register of legal English. The problems are, first of all, to do with the abbreviated spellings: *pce* for 'piece', *Psh* for 'Parish', *cold* for 'coloured', and so on. Then there is the use of the specialized vocabulary of legal English mentioned earlier, for example *aforesaid* and *there-under*. If these two obstacles have been overcome, there is a third problem concerning the grammatical organization of the text. The extract is just a part of a very long sentence that starts *It was witnessed that . . . the Vendor conveyed unto the Purchaser ALL THAT pce of land . . .* and continues for over a full typed page. However, the grammar is perfectly Standard, yet suffi-ciently unusual to make it appear non-Standard.

This extract illustrates the point that Standard English is not a simple concept, and that, with the notion of 'Standard', there are many different registers or types of English, some of which can be very difficult to understand, particularly for a lay person.

2f

BLITZ – NO TIME TO GROW UP

Mark Honingsbaum explains the passing of the decade of style.

BLITZ'S announcement last week that it was 'suspending publication' indefinitely may not be the end of the Soho-based monthly (it may yet find a wealthy backer), but it is certainly the end of that peculiarly eighties concept – the 'style' magazine. The fact is that the media-savvy 20-somethings of the Thatcher boom years have turned 30-something and begun to feel the pinch. Their collective belt-tightening threatens to bring down not only Blitz but its style-conscious competitors – the Face, Sky and iD.

The writing has been on the wall for some time now. The style press actually started dying when newspapers like this one launched their own style pages. At Blitz we knew this, which is why as the eighties ended, we promised our readers a new-look magazine which wouldn't patronize them any longer. We aimed to grow up with our readers and in so doing hoped to be around to define the new decade. We even put 'the magazine of the nineties' on the masthead.

Now we have got egg on our face and the Face and iD, who stuck with a tried and tested formula, must be crowing.
(Guardian, 2 September 1991)

This short piece of journalism illustrates yet another facet of Standard English: its ability to incorporate the ephemeral jargon of a particular generation or 'in-group'. Grammatically, the piece is written in Standard English; there are no dialect forms. But to readers who are outside the 'style' group, the use of terms like *media-savvy*, *20-somethings* or *style formula* might create problems of comprehension. It is the use of particular vocabulary items within a basically Standard set of choices that marks the piece as addressed to an in-group audience.

2.4   Implications for teaching

Standard English (both spoken and written) is, therefore, the language used to communicate to a wider, non-regional, public audience. Teachers need to recognize its social and educational importance, while at the same time respecting, and building upon, the language background of their students. Students need to take full advantage of the wide variety of lines of communication available to them, ranging from the language uses within the family and local community to those of the wider areas of community and public life.

Recent debate on the teaching of English has highlighted the need for explicit teaching of Standard English, but, as this section has argued, such an aim is not as easy as it seems. There is no doubt that teachers clearly have a responsibility to teach children to communicate in Standard Written English and to appreciate the variety, subtlety and flexibility of its forms. There is, however, a bigger problem with the teaching of Standard Spoken English – the imposition of a 'capital' language on a 'mountain' language:

In Britain, Standard English is a central issue of language in education, since Standard English is a variety of language which can be defined only by its role in the education system. It is also an example of a topic which requires careful conceptual analysis, since there is enormous confusion about terms such as 'standard', 'correct', 'proper', 'good', 'grammatical', 'academic' etc English, and such terms, are at the centre of much debate over English in education.

The question concerning the explicit teaching of Standard Written English, and the usefulness, or indeed possibility, of similarly teaching spoken patterns, will be further addressed in subsequent chapters.

SUMMARY

- The concept of Standard English needs careful and systematic investigation.
- The very word 'standard' has a variety of different meanings and connotations which can inform our understanding of its use in 'Standard' English.
- Attitudes to the concept of Standard English are deeply rooted in people's personal prejudices.
- There is, in fact, a wide variety of 'Standard' forms of English.
- Standard English concerns itself specifically with the grammatical and vocabulary forms of the language, and is not related to accent.
- Standard English (both spoken and written) is the language used to communicate to a wider, non-regional, public audience.

3 English and other Englishes

'Na, na,' says a voice above him . . . 'Pardon?' asks Petworth . . . 'You smirk,' says the stewardess. 'No,' says Petworth, looking down at the paper, 'I didn't smirk.' 'Da, you smirk,' says the stewardess, snatching the unlit cigarette from his mouth and showing it to him. 'Of course you smirk. Smirking here not permitted.' 'I'm sorry,' says Petworth. 'Only permitted is having a sweet,' says the stewardess.

There are voices, strange voices, singing in Petworth's head, the words of an English that is not quite English, English as a medium of international communication.

Words are spilling through his mind, in strange excess, a medley of sounding voices that penetrate and confuse. But it is as Katya Princip . . . has said to him . . . the more words, the more country. But what country is it? The English that is no longer English, the English of second language users, reels through his head, a head that hardly feels like his.

Malcolm Bradbury, *Rates of Exchange*
(pp. 30–31, 269, 272)

3.1 International English

One conclusion reached in the previous chapter is that Standard English is not a permanently fixed variety of English; it varies according to the contexts in which it is used and the purposes for which users of the language deploy it. It is thus preferable to consider the notion of Standard English as plural rather than singular, that is, to speak in terms of Standard Englishes rather than in terms of Standard English. In this chapter the main aim is to consider the regional, national and international dimensions to the notion of Standard Englishes. Moving beyond the boundaries of Britain and of British English also involves inevitable comparison between Standard Englishes and other languages.

ACTIVITY

This activity helps us to consider a situation outside Britain in which issues of English language use are central.

You live in a country in the Far East. This country, previously a British colony, is now independent but remains a member of the Commonwealth. There is to be a debate in parliament concerning Government plans for a more extensive development of English in schools. In particular this involves schemes to make Standard British English a medium of instruction in all schools from age eight. Some MPs have objections and argue for a retention of the national language (mother tongue for 80 per cent of the population) as the main language in school. Other MPs also argue against Standard British English and for more liberal attitudes towards a local dialect of English that is used in the country as a lingua franca.

You are asked to brief an as yet undecided MP. Complete all the slots in the following table and then work in groups to prepare either a briefing paper or an oral report on the main issues. In discussing the advantages and disadvantages of different 'languages' pay particular attention to contexts of use – that is, in what places and for what purposes the language would be used. Furthermore, do not omit to recognize that choosing one language rather than another sends particular social and/or cultural meanings between the language users. For example, to choose the national majority language sends different social

CHOOSING A LANGUAGE OF INSTRUCTION FOR SCHOOLS IN NON-NATIVE CONTEXTS				
Language	Likely contexts of use	Advantages	Disadvantages	Social and cultural meanings of the choice
National language				
Standard British English				
Local English dialect				
Other local languages				

47

signals from the choice of other local languages; it could, for example, be interpreted as an attempt by the majority to dominate the minority socially and culturally.

Some basic facts about the role of English in the world should be noted:
— there are 750 million regular speakers of English in the world, of which 300 million are native speakers;
— three-quarters of the world's mail is written in English. About 40 per cent of business deals are made in English. Eighty-five per cent of published scientific books and journals are in English;
— although there are more native speakers of Chinese than of English, English is the major language of international communication.

Arguments against further promotion of English:
— a national language is a language with which people can identify. Promoting a national language confirms people's belief in themselves, by means of a language which is <u>theirs</u>, not the imposed language of others;
— teaching and using English more extensively signals a return to a colonial past. It will not assist the process of national self-definition; indeed it compromises indigenous cultural values;
— the national language would be demoted as a medium of creative expression;
— retaining the national language as a medium of instruction in schools more effectively supports learning. Making children use English in all subject lessons can interfere with their learning;
— it is expensive. Expatriate teachers and teacher trainers would need to be employed from overseas. New investment in books, examinations etc would be needed.

Arguments for the further promotion of English:

— if it is not to be internationally isolated, the country has to recognize the increasingly vital functions of English as an international language. (Many of these functions are performed in Standard English, not in localized versions of English);

— the country needs access to networks of communication with other countries. An extension to the public uses of Standard English encourages further investment in the country by multinational companies. It allows access for all the people to the kinds of knowledge which are only available through the medium of Standard English. The country has to pay the necessary educational, social, cultural and financial price;

— it does not matter whether Standard British or Standard American English is chosen, but Commonwealth ties will ensure greater British government support for, and investment in, Standard British English;

— using Standard English as the main medium of instruction in schools gives access to a mutually intelligible international language. Local Englishes may become intelligible only within defined geographical boundaries.

One conclusion might be to recognize the existence of the different Englishes and to teach pupils to switch between local and international Englishes, as well as between English and other languages, as the context demands. Pupils thus add a Standard English to their repertoire; their range of language choice is increased, and no one version of English is automatically superior. How far is this practicable? What difficulties, if any, could you anticipate?

The discussion so far emphasizes the importance of Standard English as a medium of intra-national and international communication and underlines the significance of social, cultural and psychological factors in the choices made by nations and individuals to use Standard English. However, the reversion here to the singular term, Standard English, begs not only the major ideological question of which Standard English to choose but also the question of the linguistic consequences of choosing one rather than another.

3.2   International Englishes

This may not seem an especially problematic issue, for American, Australian and British English speakers do not normally have difficulty in communicating with one another. There are none the less a number of variations between the different Englishes.

ACTIVITY

Make a list of:
— vocabulary differences
— grammatical differences
between two international Standard Englishes with which you are familiar. Try to list at least <u>ten</u> vocabulary differences and at least <u>five</u> main grammatical differences.

Two major world Englishes are British and American, and due to news media and films these may be the most familiar. Some significant differences between these varieties are:

VOCABULARY DIFFERENCES

British English		**American English**	
petrol	rubbish (bin)	gas	garbage
nappies	trousers	diapers	pants
cupboard	post	closet	mail
tap	autumn	faucet	fall
boot (in a car)		trunk	

GRAMMATICAL DIFFERENCES

British English	American English
They'd got it	They'd gotten it
He dived into the lake	He dove into the lake
Do you have any fresh salmon?	Have you fresh salmon?
Yes, we have	Yes, we do

Of course, differences extend beyond the levels of grammar and vocabulary. For example, spellings and stress patterns vary between American and British English:

SPELLING AND STRESS DIFFERENCES

British English	American English
defence	defense
colour	color
theatre	theater
am<u>a</u>teur	<u>am</u>ateur
alum<u>in</u>ium	al<u>u</u>minum

(These three examples drawn from Trudgill and Hannah 1982)

(The latter example is of a stress <u>and</u> spelling difference. We should also note that common words do not necessarily embrace common meanings. For example, 'Don't get mad at me!' has the meaning in American English of <u>anger</u> and not the British English meaning of <u>madness</u> and mental instability. (It is interesting to observe that, perhaps due to the influence of American films and television programmes, the former usage is becoming more prevalent in British English.)

There are also differences between American and British English on one side and Australian English on the other. Although speakers of these Englishes use English as native speakers, there are none the less words and phrases that are unique to their particular kind of English. For example, in British English, footpath refers to a path across fields or through woods, while pavement refers to a pathway beside a road or street. In Australian English, however, footpath covers both. In Australian English, to barrack for a team means 'to express support', whereas in British English the same term means 'to shout abuse or unfavourable comment'.

Furthermore, within British English there are grammatical and lexical differences between the Standard English spoken in the three countries that make up Britain. Here are some features which differentiate Standard Scottish English from Standard English English:

Standard Scottish English	Standard English English
Vocabulary	
loch	lake
burn	stream
bairn/wain	child
outwith	outside
wee	small
Grammar	
You had a good time, hadn't you?	You had a good time, didn't you?
Did you buy one yet?	Have you bought one yet?
Will I tell her?	Shall I tell her?

We might conclude at this stage that there is indeed no such thing as Standard English and that it is more realistic, both linguistically and culturally, to accept the existence of many different varieties of English and to speak in terms of Standard Englishes rather than Standard English. The discussion in this section does, however, raise questions. For example:

— how significant are the differences between Standard Englishes? Do they result in serious breakdowns in communication? In spite of differences, do Standard Englishes actually share more common features than they have features which differentiate them?

— are differences between Englishes more salient in spoken than in written versions of the language?

— what are the implications for the teaching of English as a mother tongue or as a second or foreign language if learners come into regular contact, often in informal spoken contexts, with varieties of English which are unique to them as members of a family, region or country?

3.3 Regional variation and non-native Englishes

In the remainder of this chapter, answers to the above questions are sought by looking in greater detail at more localized varieties of English. We shall examine examples of British English in different geographical regions; in other words we will examine some examples of <u>dialectal</u> variation in British English. We shall also look at further examples of variation in English internationally, though with a focus on English in use by speakers for whom English is either a second or foreign language rather than, as in 3.1 and 3.2, by speakers for whom English is a mother tongue.

The following list illustrates some common features of local dialects of British English. (The list is extracted from Trudgill

1983 and Edwards 1984.) How significant are these differences?
Is it true to say that there is more common ground than
differences between the dialects of the language, including the

VERBS	EXAMPLE	SE EQUIVALENT
Present tense		
1. Sometimes these differ from the standard	I <u>wants</u> it (Reading dialect)	I <u>want</u> it
Past tense		
1. Some verbs have the same present- and past-tense forms	I <u>give</u> it to him yesterday	I <u>gave</u> it to him yesterday
2. Some verbs have the same form for past participle and past tense	You <u>done</u> it, did you?	You <u>did</u> it, did you?
3. 'Weren't' is sometimes used with 'I' and 's/he'	I <u>weren't</u> going there	I <u>wasn't</u> going there
Modal		
1. Sometimes these differ from the standard	I <u>oughtn't</u> to say that (West Yorkshire dialect)	I <u>shouldn't</u> say that

NEGATION	EXAMPLE	SE EQUIVALENT
1. Multiple negation is generally the rule in British dialects	I <u>don't</u> eat <u>none</u> of that	I <u>don't</u> eat <u>any</u> of that
2. 'Ain't' (sometimes pronounced 'ent' or 'int') – the negative present of 'be'	It <u>ain't</u> that big	It <u>isn't</u> that big
3. 'Never' as a past tense negative	She did yesterday, but she <u>never</u> today	She did yesterday, but she <u>didn't</u> today
4. 'Ain't' – the negative of 'have'	We <u>ain't</u> got one	We <u>haven't</u> got one
5. 'No' or 'nae' as negative	She's <u>no</u> there (Scottish dialect)	She's <u>not</u> there

PRONOUNS	EXAMPLE	SE EQUIVALENT
Relative		
1. 'What' and 'which' (for non-humans) used in dialect in place of 'who' (for humans)	Are you the one <u>what</u> said it?	Are you the one <u>who</u> said it?
Personal		
1. These occasionally differ in non-Standard forms	Are <u>youse</u> coming? (Belfast dialect, for plural 'you')	Are <u>you</u> coming?
Reflexive		
1. 'Hisself' and 'theirselves' are occasionally found in non-Standard forms	He did it <u>hisself</u>	He did it <u>himself</u>

DEMONSTRATIVES	EXAMPLE	SE EQUIVALENT
1. 'Them' and 'they' often correspond to the Standard form 'those'	Over by <u>them</u> bus-stops	Over by <u>those</u> bus-stops

PREPOSITIONS	EXAMPLE	SE EQUIVALENT
1. Prepositions of place sometimes differ in non-Standard forms	It was <u>at</u> London	It was <u>in</u> London
2. 'Up' sometimes occurs without 'to'	I went <u>up</u> London	I went <u>up</u> to London

NOUNS OF MEASUREMENT	EXAMPLE	SE EQUIVALENT
1. Very often there is no plural marking in non-Standard forms	She walked thirteen <u>mile</u>	She walked thirteen <u>miles</u>

ADVERBS	EXAMPLE	SE EQUIVALENT
1. Adverbs sometimes have the same form as adjectives	He did it <u>nice</u>	He did it <u>nicely</u>

COMPARATIVES AND SUPERLATIVES	EXAMPLE	SE EQUIVALENT
1. Many dialects allow both 'more'/'most' and '-er'/ -'est' simultaneously	She gets <u>more rougher</u>	She gets <u>rougher</u>
	He's the <u>most tallest</u> person I know	He's the <u>tallest</u> person I know

dialect of Standard British English, and that it is more useful to recognize this common ground than to highlight the differences? Note: These examples can be used as a framework for identifying the main areas of difference in the dialects of particular regions, and can be usefully operated by students of all ages.

It is interesting to note that the different dialects of British English would appear to have more in common with one another than they have in common with the dialect of Standard English. For example, double and multiple negation are prevalent in many of the dialects of British English <u>except</u> in the dialect of Standard English, and to some extent <u>this</u> fact explains the salience of this feature when it appears in non-Standard usage, the corresponding function of this and other such forms as linguistic shibboleths within British society, and the outlawing of such forms from all authorized versions of the English language. It is ironic, of course, that double negation is 'correct' in many world languages (for example, French and Russian) and cannot therefore be dismissed as a speech illogicality of the uneducated. And there are also certain forms of double negation that are a natural and normal part of a legitimized Standard

English: for example, in the sentence I am not uninterested in your proposal, double negation, constructed around an adjective rather than around a verbal group, is a common way of expressing a cautious and noncommittal position.

A further interesting point to note is that the examples of non-Standard forms listed here are unlikely to cause fundamental difficulties of comprehension. There may, of course, be difficulties caused by the accent associated with the forms, but the same may also apply to communication through Standard English, since Standard English may be spoken with any accent. There are certainly no insuperable decoding difficulties.

The following list illustrates some features of local Englishes – examples drawn from international usages of English in which the users are normally non-native speakers of English. It is interesting to note here the extent to which comprehension difficulties may be caused by the variations.

Usage	Locality of use	SE equivalent
He is knowing her very well	Indian, Malaysian, West African	He knows her very well
She is having a headache		She has a headache
I am doubting it		I doubt it
This house – too small	Indian, Singaporean	This house is too small
My sister – in London		My sister is in London
That – the second car I have		That's my second car
This man brother	Caribbean	This man's brother
You want David, is it?	Indian	You want David, do you?
You're not going home, is it?	Malaysian/Singaporean	You're not going home, are you?
To have hard ears	Caribbean	To be stubborn or disobedient
To open the radio	Philippine	To turn on the radio
To put sand in someone's gari	East African	To threaten someone's livelihood

(Examples drawn from Platt, Weber and Ho 1984)

The examples here parallel those provided in section 3.2, where some differences in native international Englishes were distinguished; and the linguistic implications of such differences and distinctions remain similar. Some vocabulary items are variety-specific (for example, gari, in the final example, is a kind of cassava flour used as a staple food in southern Nigeria); other items can be decoded by inference or by reference to the surrounding linguistic context. Syntactic differences do not constitute particular difficulties, and indeed are characterized by a uniformity which once again underlines that the Standard language deviates more markedly from the non-Standard or local forms than such forms differ intrinsically from one another. We might note finally that vocabulary and accent differences are more likely than syntactic differences to result in lack of comprehension, and that contexts of spoken usage allow greater opportunities for any necessary disambiguation or clarification than is normally the case with written usage.

Some conclusions can be drawn at this stage; the points raised here will be explored further in subsequent chapters, but discussion of examples and issues so far leads to the following main points of conclusion. First, standard languages, however arbitrarily they may have arisen or however much they may have been imposed by colonial exigencies, do serve a key function of providing a largely agreed and codified version of the language for purposes of national and international communication. The grammar and vocabulary of the different international Englishes are relatively homogeneous and provide an existing base for communication in the written language and in formal contexts of spoken language use. Second, it is necessary therefore to emphasize the importance of teaching and learning Standard English. Third, variation cannot be lightly dismissed or ignored. There are certainly dangers that variation can lead to some difficulties of communication; that, in the absence of a codified, standardized version of the language, different varieties can result in excessively fragmented forms; and that, in such a situation, English may, rather like Latin, cease to function as an international language in the future. The evidence is, however, that differences are exaggerated and that an excessively homogeneous version of the language, if adopted inflexibly, can lead to losses in identity which are of both personal and psychological, as well as regional and national, significance.

3.4 The position of the writer

This final point can be briefly re-emphasized with reference to the position of writers who have chosen to adopt English as a medium of creative expression even though it is not for them a native language. Two contrasting views are expressed below by writers who have made major international contributions to literatures written in English:

So my answer to the question: Can an African ever learn English well enough to be able to use it effectively in creative writing? Is certainly yes. If on the other hand you ask: Can he ever learn to use it like a native speaker? I should say, I hope not. It is neither necessary nor desirable for him to be able to do so. The price a world language must be prepared to pay is submission to many different kinds of use. The African writer should aim to use English in a way that brings out his message best without altering the language to the extent that its value as a medium of international exchange will be lost. He should aim at fashioning out an English which is at once universal and able to carry his peculiar experience ... It will have to be a new English, still in full communion with its ancestral home, but altered to suit its new African surroundings. (Achebe 1965)

The oppressed and the exploited of the earth maintain their defiance: liberty from theft. But the biggest weapon wielded and actually daily unleashed by imperialism against that collective defiance is the cultural bomb. The effect of a cultural bomb is to annihilate a people's belief in their names, in their languages, in their environment, in their heritage of struggle, in their unity, in their capacities and ultimately in them-selves. It makes them see their past as one wasteland of non-achievement and it makes them want to distance themselves from that wasteland. It makes them want to identify with that which is furthest removed from themselves; for instance, with other people's languages rather than their own. (Thiong 1981)

These statements also underline that discussions of language cannot be neutral, that the choice of a language in such a context is an ideological choice, and that issues of personal identity are inextricably connected with uses of English, both nationally and internationally.

A final word in this chapter can be left to Nissim Ezekiel, who uses a poem in Indian English as a medium for encapsulating something of the ambivalences which are created by the existence of Standard and non-Standard Englishes. What is the purpose of Ezekiel's use of language? For purposes of comedy and ironic self-deprecation, or as an authentic, linguistically revealing ex-pression of the non-native English writer's dilemma?

> I am standing for peace and non-violence
> Why world is fighting fighting
> Why all people of world
> Are not following Mahatma Gandhi
> I am simply not understanding.
> Ancient Indian Wisdom is 100% correct.
> I should say even 200% correct.
> But Modern generation is neglecting –
> Too much going for fashion and foreign thing.

(Ezekiel 1982)

SUMMARY

- It is important that Standard English is viewed from an international perspective and is not simply regarded as of relevance only to a single nation or to separate nations. With the wider view, the notion of Englishes rather than English emerges.

- Standard English is clearly of national and international use, though there are real dangers if it is adopted indiscriminately and inflexibly.

- As a national or international dialect, Standard English is predominantly associated with the written language and with formal contexts of use. The rules of Standard English, including those for spelling and punctuation, are codified and vary little from one Standard English to another.

- For purposes of teaching, teachers need to prepare pupils so that they know how and when to use Standard English and know the contexts in which non-Standard forms are more appropriate and meaningful.

- Although Standard Englishes share a common code, non-Standard forms share much in common and are often neither incomprehensible, illogical nor illegitimate. They are a key fact of a user's identity.

- A Standard language provides a largely agreed version of the language for national and international communication.

4   It ain't what you say

I don't think at most schools nowadays they teach elocution so there does tend to be an inability to pronounce actual syllables as correctly and crisply as they ought to be . . . So far as speech is concerned I would like to see a reintroduction of elocution as a definite subject. I was taught elocution at school very well and I enjoyed learning it, and it's stood me in good stead ever since.

Paul Johnson, *The Late Show*, BBC2, December 1993

One of the recurring themes of this book has been the need to see all language in relation to the uses to which it is put and the contexts in which it occurs. In connection with this view we have recognized that there is considerable variation between spoken and written usage. Judgements of what is 'good' or 'correct' or 'Standard' English do not always take sufficient account of differences between speech and writing.

A Yorkshireman wanted an inscription on his wife's gravestone. He felt that 'She Was Thine' would be sufficient, and instructed the mason accordingly. However, the engraver made a mistake and the finished result read 'She Was Thin'. The Yorkshireman wrote to the mason pointing out that the 'E' had been missed out. The mason got to work again. The amended result read: 'E, She Was Thin'.

The nature of the humour rests solely on the spoken form of dialect usage, in relation to its written context.

One basic judgement which remains constant is that RP

accents are inseparable from Standard English, when in fact Standard English can be spoken in any accent. However, differences between speech and writing in English are often more fundamental.

4.1 Spoken and written language

ACTIVITY

The following sentences are taken from texts produced by children aged 11 to 14. They were collected during a study of language teaching and development for the LINC (Language in the National Curriculum) Project. Which sentences do you think have been extracted from predominantly spoken contexts and which from predominantly written contexts? Give reasons. Rank the sentences in order from 'most likely to be spoken' to 'most likely to be written'.

4a

1. *We've, erm, sort of decided not to.*
2. *There's a few problems are likely to crop up.*
3. *The women all shouted.*
4. *The women they all shouted.*
5. *Opportunities can be created at short notice.*
6. *It was good that book.*
7. *That was a good book.*
8. *What I want to say is . . . is that he couldn't have, you know, like, been the murderer, I mean the assassin.*
9. *It has been decided to refer the problem to the authorities.*
10. *That house on the corner, is that where you live?*

(Author's data)

Examples 1 and 8 are unambiguously spoken in that the written representation indicates the hesitations, false starts and changes in direction and language choice associated with ongoing speech. The sentences also contain fillers such as *like* or *you know*, which serve both to allow time to think and to check that sufficient shared knowledge is established. Other phrases, such as *I mean* or *sort of*, similarly allow the speaker respectively to reformulate and to moderate what is being said. Examples 5 and 9 are more conspicuously written in style; the presence of passive (*It has been decided/can be created*) normally indicates that the language is more likely to be written than spoken.

But what about the other sentences? Some could be either written or spoken: for example, sentences 3 and 7. And what of examples 4 and 6? Examples 4 and 6 are modelled on examples 3 and 7. Are they 'grammatical'? Are they Standard English?

As we have seen, the history of the description of English grammar and its properties has been the history of the description of English grammar as it has occurred in the written language. Correct grammar has thus, by definition, come to mean correct grammar as judged by that version of English represented by the written language. This situation has roots in the lexicography of the eighteenth century, when Dr Samuel Johnson excluded entries from his *Dictionary of the English Language* which were not attested in written literary sources, on the grounds that they constituted no more than ephemeral vulgarisms. Such a view of language explains to some extent why, in mother-tongue language education at least, writing and reading carry greater prestige than speaking – a situation rigorously reinforced by the National Curriculum for English in England and Wales, with its deliberate and very public downgrading of spoken language competence. But it surfaces in an even more complex form in arguments over what is 'correct' and what is 'Standard' English. The popular and prevailing view is that correct English grammar is what is codified in grammars of English; yet what is codified in English grammars does not tell the whole story. One teaching outcome of such circular discussion is that there are dangers, in both EMT and EFL/ESL domains, of producing speakers of English who speak like a book because their English is modelled on an almost exclusively written version of the language.

4.2   Grammar and errors

Recent research into the spoken language (facilitated by rapid improvements in audio technology), and the compilation of ever richer databases of spoken English, is drawing our attention to forms of the language not so far described in most standard grammars of English. Here are some of the most frequently recurring examples:

— *It was good that book. / It was a good film that one.*

in which a pronoun or noun phrase is repeated co-referentially.

— *The women they all shouted. / The man over there he said it was OK.*

in which a left-displaced noun phrase subject is immediately followed by a 'recapitulatory' pronoun.

— *There's a few problems are likely to crop up.*

in which the main verb is repeated in a structure in which initial-subject/verb concord is rare.

— *That house on the corner, is that where you live?*

in which an anticipatory, 'clarificatory' phrase precedes an interrogative.

Most of these examples (and scores more could be listed) reflect the essentially interpersonal nature of the spoken language, with the structures often serving in particular to clarify, to contextualize, or to establish shared knowledge and frames of reference in ways which are either impossible or unnecessary in the written language. Yet it is not difficult to imagine situations in which such structures could be declared to be non-Standard, ungrammatical English (even though frequently used by speakers of Standard English) because standard grammars of the language exclude them from the range of canonical forms. Certainly few EFL reference grammars or coursebooks appear to concede the existence of such structures, although no criticism of such materials is possible since once again we can only work from those descriptions that are available.

SUMMARY

- Differences between speech and writing in English are very apparent, and need to be seen in the context of Standard and non-Standard English uses.
- English grammar is based primarily on the written language, and does not take sufficient account of spoken contexts of use.
- The nature of spoken language is essentially interpersonal.

5 Reflecting on language use

A major unanswered and unexplained question in knowledge about language for pupils concerns the relationship between knowledge about or reflection on language and a development of competence in the use of language ... What can be said is that pupils are likely to benefit from detailed consideration being given to the forms and function of language variation. Such is the importance of an ability to control language in all its many variations that the more angles that can be provided on those variations the better.

> R. Carter, *Knowledge about Language and the Curriculum*

Two 7-year-olds, Marc and Jamie, discuss their first draft of a story about life on a pig farm. They are rereading the text together and discussing its effect:

Marc: '*the pig ran across the farmyard. Suddenly she heard the noise.*' *The noise – that's not right – it should be a noise.*
Jamie: *why?*
Marc: *because, if it was the noise, the pig would have been expecting it.*

During the past ten years or so there has been an increase of interest, on the part of English language teachers, in the value of encouraging pupils to reflect on uses of language, both their own uses and those of others. Such practices have been developed because teachers have felt the need to talk more explicitly about language with their pupils. There has been no desire to extend or return to a mechanistic, decontextualized analysis of language forms (associated, in part, with English teaching in Britain in the 1950s, and reintroduced in the English textbooks outlined in the Introduction), but there has been a willingness to develop procedures for stimulating greater awareness of how language works, particularly in the construction of texts. Marc and Jamie's opportunity to <u>talk</u> about the text they have produced involves a perceptive discussion of the role of different language features (that is, <u>the</u>: 'serving to particularize as needing no further identification' (*Oxford Reference Dictionary*); and <u>a</u>: 'one person or thing but not any specific one' (*Oxford Reference Dictionary*).) Although extensive research evidence has yet to be produced, many teachers believe that there is a connection between pupils' explicit discussion of language and their capacity to produce and use language accurately and appropriately.

In the teaching of modern foreign languages these procedures have been termed courses in **language awareness** (see Donmall 1985). In the context of mother-tongue English teaching the term KAL (**Knowledge About Language**) has been preferred and, indeed, this is the term promoted by the Cox Committee (DES 1989) in a working-party report on English in the National Curriculum in England and Wales. In the teaching of English as a second or foreign language, the development of programmes for language awareness has run parallel with the development of learner training materials (see Ellis and Sinclair 1989, McCarthy and Carter 1994, chapter 4). In this chapter it is argued that the promotion of greater knowledge about language and, preferably, greater reflection on language can be an effective way of fostering an improved understanding among all learners of English of the specific styles, purposes and variety of spoken and written Standard Englishes.

5.1   Talking about talk

This activity is designed to help you explore your own percep-
tions of the nature of language investigation and description.
The aim is to develop a provisional framework for investigating
language that might be used to assist pupils' investigations
of their own and others' uses of language.

Work in groups of two or three to investigate some ways in
which we 'begin' talk. If possible, tape-record some specific
examples of conversational openings. Try to collect data in
contexts which contrast with one another; for example, compare
and contrast openings to interviews with openings to lessons, or
openings to telephone conversations with initiating 'small talk'
at a social gathering.

Investigation should ideally proceed through three main stages:

Collection: in which actual data and examples are collected.
List actual examples of language use: various kinds of greeting;
self-identification; different types of question and answer; functions of phatic talk (for example, talking about the weather as a
means of initial social contact); explanation (or the absence of
it) of the reasons for the talk.

Comparison: in which the differences in the data are con-
trasted and compared in terms of the social setting, the purpose
of the talk and the social relationship of the participants.

Classification: in which attempts are made to classify or
otherwise label the data in terms of its functions and its differing
levels of formality. Analysis of particular forms and structures of
language should be related to their functions and purposes.

Thus, a basic framework of collection, comparison and classification is established. So, for example, in terms of exploring
'beginning talk', the investigation might well start with simply

listing examples produced in a particular situation (for example, starting the morning: 'Time to get up', 'Aren't you gerring up?', 'Turn the alarm off', 'Breakfast's on t'table', 'See ya!', 'Hurry up!'. Collecting the utterances then leads to comparing one with another in terms of their form and function, thereby producing a means of classifying their similarities and differences, in the following ways:

— the formality/informality of the relationship or situation
— the notion of turn-taking
— male/female comparisons
— the use of Standard/non-Standard forms.

Above all, it is important to stress the need for the investigation to move from collecting data to classifying it, rather than starting with pre-formulated labels for describing the talk. The level of detail in which comparisons and classifications are made will vary according to the teacher's assessment of learning needs, but the stages are relevant to learners at all levels, from primary-school native speakers to advanced learners of English as a foreign language.

What now follows in 5.2 and 5.3 is a variety of language-based tasks that can be explored using this system.

5.2   Investigating language (a case-study)

Over the last couple of years, a group of teachers from primary schools on the south-eastern edge of the inner city in Sheffield, England, have been exploring different aspects of talk with pupils in their classes. This has involved them in:

— planning for different kinds of talk to be used;
— being more explicit about the purposes of classroom talk;
— asking children to be more reflective about their own talk and the range and variety of talk they hear around them.

One activity the group tried recently was to ask their pupils –

ranging from Reception Year 1 through to Year 7 (ages 5 to 12) – to think about the kinds of talk that went on in different parts of their classroom and school. With the youngest children this took the form of groups collaboratively working on large drawings of the classroom and adding – or getting the teacher to add – 'balloons' containing bits of typical classroom talk or dialogue. They displayed an awareness of a large range of talk around the whole school. Children were seen:

— arguing ('Get lost', 'Stop swearing');
— informing ('Me dad's picking me up', 'Someone's scribbled in the book');
— greeting ('Hello', 'Good morning');
— making requests ('Can I have seconds?', 'Can I play?');
— questioning ('What time is it?', 'Have you got this book?');
— playing together (playground chants).

They also revealed an awareness of the flexibility of language use according to situation; for example, 'me dad's picking me up' – an informal, non-Standard usage for one child talking to another.

Adults were shown to be involved in a similar range of talk, either with children or among themselves; these included the headteacher, school secretary, dinner ladies, caretaker, ice-cream-van driver, parents and teachers.

As well as being an activity in which children could operate as 'experts', this gave an opportunity for discussion of how talk changes according to whom you talk ('We talk to our friends differently because we have to be polite to you'; 'You wouldn't say these to Mrs . . . [headteacher] 'cos they're not nice to say'). In the longer term, of course, it is part of a process by which talk comes to be recognized as a crucial part of language development, on a par with reading and writing in terms of the National Curriculum in England and Wales. Talk is an area in which young children already have considerable knowledge and control, and teachers need to help them both to value what they already have and to see talk as something worthy of investigation in its own right.

With the older classes, mainly Years 6 and 7 (ages 11 to 12), groups of pupils were either provided with a basic plan of the school or produced one themselves, and again were asked to think about the different kinds of talk that went on. A wide range of purposes and styles appeared, though with greater evidence of subject matter being confined to distinct parts of the school – romantic gossip exclusively in the toilets and on the playing-field! In many cases the maps extended beyond the school to include local shops, houses and other buildings, and here pupils not only revealed the variety and depth of their insights into local life, but a very clear awareness of accent and dialect being used in appropriate situations. Settings included:

— the old people's home ('Nobody comes to see me');
— the bus-stop ('Oh, no, I haven't got no change'; 'They're always late');
— the shops ('This flour costs a bomb'; 'Yes, love, wait a minute');
— the pub ('Another pint please, mate'; 'Same again, Fred');
— the post office ('I've come about me pension');
— the betting-shop ('Red Rum'll never win'; 'I bet he will');
— home ('Get up and get ready for school'; 'Oh, do I have to');
— the street ('Flipping Sunday drivers!'; 'Morning, luv').

In one class, the groups, when they had worked on their maps, were asked to look at the range of talk they had identified and try to come up with some general categories; this approach is similar to the collect–compare–classify model suggested earlier. Following discussion, a list of categories was compiled by the class (for example, suggesting, complaining, informing, joking, commanding, asking) and groups were then asked to apply them to the talk they had put on their maps and see where particular kinds of talk occurred.

As with the younger groups, the activity allows pupils to share knowledge in which they are the experts and provides a context for discussion of many aspects of talk, both in and out of school. It helps challenge simplistic notions of 'good' and 'bad' language by suggesting that different kinds of talk are appropriate in different situations, and it indicates to pupils that they can reflect on the range of audiences and purposes for talk in the same way that they do for writing and reading.

5.3 Investigating further

The following are suggestions for investigating contexts of spoken or written language use in the classroom, where the collect–compare–classify model of investigation might well apply.

1. The Programmes of Study for Speaking and Listening at Key Stage 1 in the National Curriculum in England and Wales suggest that activities should 'develop speaking and listening skills, both when role-playing and otherwise'. Several infant schools in Barnsley in the county of Yorkshire, England, have now set up carefully planned role-play areas in the classroom, providing opportunities for even very young children to explore, and reflect upon, the different talk registers they use, and to discuss them in relation to their reading of a variety of different forms of writing.

A visit to a local supermarket may lead to one being set up in the classroom. This involves the children in creating, and commenting upon, a variety of different activities: producing posters, adverts, competition leaflets, shopping lists; creating customer service areas where forms need to be filled in for refunds, complaints, etc.; providing space for 'special promotions' (for example, cereals, fruit juice etc). Children, in role-play, may be customers (fathers, mothers, children, grandparents), check-out personnel, customer service personnel, shelf-stackers or management.

Both the setting up of the area and its use can involve the children in reflecting upon the kinds of language used: the form, purpose and audience for the different kinds of writing; the different kinds of talk they use in their role-play activities in, for example, the supermarket; what kinds of reading are involved.

The use of such areas in the classroom (be it supermarket, corner shop, travel agent, newsagent or chip shop) will naturally build on pupils' implicit knowledge about language. Creating such contexts for language use can then, quite naturally, lead to situations where the teacher might give children the opportunity to talk about, and reflect on, the nature of the language used in such situations; for example, why do you, as a cashier, talk to a customer like that? What did you read as you went around the supermarket? From language use we move to explicit reflection on what language we use, and why we use it.

2. Other activities that primary and secondary schools have found useful in providing opportunities for children to reflect on language use can be broadly grouped in two distinct (yet overlapping) categories: the language children use and the language others use.

The language children use

— producing a language 'map' of the school (showing the different kinds of talk, reading and writing that occur inside the school);
— compiling lists of words/phrases appropriate or inappropriate for use in different situations;
— comparing how to tell a story with how to write one;
— examining the value of group talk.

The language others use

— comparing different languages, spoken and written, used in the school;
— investigating genre-types (for example, what makes a fairy story);
— looking at how language has changed over time;
— exploring how texts (both spoken and written) vary in form according to situation and purpose.

The examples are endless, but the principle is fixed and specific: opportunities for observing, commenting on or analysing language can stem quite logically from collecting examples of its use. It will also be seen that such investigations provide a basis for enhancing pupils' understanding of the uses and functions of Standard English and, in particular, the contexts in which the use of Standard English is necessary, desirable or inappropriate. The aim is to establish links between a reflective language user and an effective language user.

5.4 Language to talk about language

Any policy document, either at primary or secondary level, needs to address the issue of the relevance of terminology: does it help children, in their exploration of language in use, to have a language to talk about language (in fact, a metalanguage)?

The National Curriculum for England and Wales refers, at times, in what appears to be a very random and haphazard way, to the need for pupils to know certain terms for talking about language. For example, programmes of study for writing state that children should be taught, in the context of discussion about their own writing, grammatical terms 'such as' <u>sentence</u>, <u>verb</u>, <u>tense</u>, <u>noun</u>, <u>pronoun</u>. That a definitive (and national) list of terms is <u>not</u> prescribed is evident in the phrase 'such as'. The focus for any discussion on using language to talk about language is clearly signalled in relation to context and language use: whatever 'terms' it might be useful for children to know are clearly only to be considered in the context of children reflecting on actual language use (both spoken and written). Sometimes children will be capable of discussing language without resorting to a metalanguage; at other times they will need one. Any school policy, therefore, needs to avoid a definitive list of terms, but needs to consider the range of terms that can be identified as using language to talk about language. For example, one primary school in Sheffield considered the following terms appropriate to introduce (where needed): <u>word</u>, <u>sentence</u>, <u>story</u>, <u>beginning</u>, <u>verb</u>, <u>pre-suffix</u> – but concluded that much depends on the individual child, the situation and whether the introduction of the term facilitates the reflection on language in use.

There are, in fact, many situations in the primary- and secondary-school classroom where there are opportunities to 'talk about language', raising awareness of the contexts in which Standard and non-Standard varieties of English are best used:

TALKING
— create a personal diary of talk used in any one day/week (What? Why?);
— tape group/pair discussions and comment on the language used;
— compare 'telling' with 'writing';
— set up language investigations (such as accent/dialect surveys; current 'in fashion' vocabulary and expressions; a comparison of the different languages used in the school).

READING
— keep a journal of what is read – but also why? How?

—compare the different kinds of text that are read (for example, signs, adverts, notices etc);

—compare how different texts are structured (for example, how different stories begin; different versions of the same story; information books on the same topic; news/media accounts of the same event);

—read and discuss as a group different texts with similar 'themes' (such as different adverts for coffee).

WRITING

—compile a personal writing diary, which notes the writing produced during a day/week, in terms of What? For whom? Why? How?

—create writing corners/structured play areas where children can have the opportunity to write in specific circumstances;

—pair/group collaborations provide opportunities for talking about texts (either written or word-processed);

—talk about writing not only in terms of its <u>form</u> (story, poem, recipe, letter etc), but also, crucially, in terms of its <u>function</u> (informing, entertaining, persuading, comparing etc) and in terms of its <u>context</u> (addressed to self, teacher, friends, local community etc).

5.5   Speaking and writing Standard English: extending language awareness

In schools involved in creating KAL contexts in the classroom, it has become evident that children come to school with an extensive implicit knowledge of language. Schools must acknowledge, and make use of, this awareness to help children, throughout their education, to become effective users of English. The following case-studies perhaps illustrate how this 'reflecting on language use' best operates in practice.

5a

M: *I'm frightened of a lot of things*

Mrs P: *yes, we all are*

M: *still . . . my Richard . . . he's frightened of a horse*

Mrs P: *is he*

M: *yes*

Mrs P: *and are you frightened of a horse*

M: *I'm not . . . I'm not frightened of it*

Mrs P: *no*

M: *one . . . one time when we were playing outside a horse came down my road . . . and Richard went running in going whoo*

Mrs P: *screaming*

M: *yes . . . you know if he ever sees a horse he says ooh dat orse will bite me . . . you know how he talks he says bu for bus and and he used to say dar for car . . . but I was . . . talk . . . say daddy's car when I was even none. Richard was saying tegluguletet and he says when he was none he says mememum an he thinks he was talking properly . . . he can say car now Richard can and he says who dat ouse . . . and he said me instead of my and when we play and Richard says me pooh in my clean naa*

Mrs P: *he says what*

M: *me pooh in my clean naa*

Mrs P: *and what does that mean*

M: *I've poohed in my clean nappy*

Mrs P: *oh dear* (both laughing)

(Ede, J. and J. Williamson 1980)

Here, 5-year-old Michael is talking to his class teacher, Mrs Parkin, during the lunch-hour. Discussion of language use can best be effected in informal situations and, in this context, it is Mrs Parkin who takes on the role of 'sympathetic listener'. It provides Michael with the opportunity to reflect on:

— the developmental linguistic progress of his younger brother, Richard, from babbling to use of words and phrases;

— the way Standard and non-Standard forms of the language are used (*me pooh in my clean naa* and *I've poohed in my clean nappy*). He becomes his own translator.

By giving Michael room to develop his ideas, his teacher sets up a situation where he is the language 'expert'.

When a group of 8-year-old Sheffield children were given the opportunity to talk about the English people use, these were some of their observations:

5b

— *the girls always talk posh to t'teachers in class*

— *Prince Charles talks posh . . . he's got a funny accent*

— *it's better than ours because it's more posher*

— *my mum talks posh when she goes to t'museum but when she's at home she doesn't – she just talks ordinary to us, my mum*

— *my dad is a bit rough – he can't talk really posh – he just goes, ah do our kid – my dad can't talk posh I don't think – I've never heard him anyway.*

(*Every Child's Language*, The Open University)

These children are obviously thinking a lot about the nature of English use, in terms of both individuals and situations. Group discussion such as this can often start children thinking about the nature of Standard and non-Standard English, in terms of their own language use as well as that of the people around them.

5c

H: *nobody said when they were asking questions, 'That's really stupid, you should've done it that way' . . .*

C: *yeah, 'You will do it this way next time' . . .*

B: yeah, they weren't being nasty, they tr . . . sort of . . . tried to say it but not . . . really . . .

H: (laughs) *More politely than usual . . .*

S: all of them tried to understand, in a way . . . to understand what you're doing.

H: sort of say, 'Well, you could've done it that way' or 'Next time, will you do it this way?', that sort of thing . . .

C: 'you could try it this way next time but if it doesn't work do it this way.'

H: (thinking back on the way her own group had worked) *I wasn't offended when Barry said, 'Well, I don't really like your idea about the boulders', I just got on with it because, well, I'm used to it now.*

C: yeah, we – we both agreed on that, so we did it.

H: (laughing) *yeah.* (pause) *So it wasn't really just my idea, it was CJ's as well.*

S: if someone does an idea that . . . I don't really . . . agree with, normally I don't actually . . . 'cause if it – if I knew that it will work, I don't actually say that isn't bad I just try and make mine . . . just make mine good instead of . . . you know, just leave them getting on with it like they . . . want to.

(*Language in the National Curriculum*, LINC)

This discussion occurs between a group of 9- to 11-year-olds. Initially, they had been engaged in solving a problem that involved removing a huge boulder blocking their path. This transcript, however, illustrates how they felt the actual task-solving situation had developed. Their teacher asked them to reflect on how 'successful' or 'unsuccessful' their collaborative discussions had been. Their comments give some insight into what they 'know' about the effective use of spoken English:

—criticisms and advice are much more likely to be accepted if they are offered tactfully: *Well, you could've done it that way;*

— insults or condemnation make people less likely to accept suggestions or criticisms: *That's really stupid*;

— offering advice as questions or as alternative possibilities, without condemning what has already been done, can be very effective: *Nobody said . . . 'That's really stupid'*; *'. . . will you do it this way?'*;

— it can be comforting and reassuring to have your ideas endorsed and supported by someone else: *So it wasn't really just my idea, it was CJ's as well.*

Encouraging children to produce their own language profiles or 'autobiographies' can, in a written form, provide them with the opportunity to reflect on the nature of English in relation to their own experience of its use. Here are examples of several language histories, both spoken and written.

5d

SOFIA

I was born in Pakistan and was two years old when we left for Uganda. I had my primary and secondary education in Kampala.

I have beautiful memories of my childhood in a beautiful country with exotic weather.

There were many different languages, religions and cultures in Uganda.

The languages I was surrounded by were mainly Urdu, Punjabi, Gujarati, Kutchi, Hindi, English and Swahili and I speak all these languages.

I learnt to speak these languages from my friends whom I used to play with in my neighbourhood.

I had to be very careful when I spoke to elders because I had to use special polite words to address them, like in Urdu I would say to my close friends 'Tuoom ke see hou?' which means 'How are you?' or 'App kese haï?' which is for elders and sounds very polite for 'How are you?' and the same applies to any other Asian language.

At home I spoke my own language and used two different structures and tone, one for my parents and one with my brothers and sisters.

Languages was not very difficult because the weather throughout the year is the same and the houses are open with ample space to play with friends.

I was also good at learning different languages and now I find them very useful in my teaching profession!

(*Language Profiles*, Hounslow Language Centre)

5e

CAROLYN: MY LANGUAGE PROFILE

I grew up in Wagga Wagga, Australia. Everyone around me had a similar accent and I thought everyone talked like me.

In high school we could learn another language. We could choose between Indonesian, German, French and Latin. I learnt French and enjoyed saying 'Bonjour Madame' to my teacher. I became a lot better at speaking French when I lived in France for 2 months.

When I went to Queensland and visited my uncle who lives on a farm, he was never in a rush and talked much slower than me. Also, in the country people spent more time chatting before they spoke about business than we did in the city.

When I came to England 6 years ago, people didn't like the way my voice went up at the end of sentences. I felt embarrassed and sometimes I felt angry. I tried to talk like the English, but I don't sound the same. Now, I like my accent.

A lot of English people think I come from New Zealand. When I visited Australia last year, people thought I sounded English.

I like it when they play <u>Neighbours</u> on TV because I like listening to Australian accents.

In Australia we used words people in England don't use, like 'G'day' for 'Good day' and 'I'm real crook' for 'I feel ill'.

I enjoyed moving to Hounslow and hearing lots of different languages and learning new things from the children in my class.

Last holiday, I went to Scotland. I like listening to the Scottish accent. We went to a party and sang 'Auld Lang Syne'.

When I talk on the phone, I sometimes use a special phone voice. It's a bit posh. When I talk to headteachers, I'm very polite and say, 'Good morning, Mrs . . .' When I talk to my friends, I say, 'Hi ya'.

(*Language Profiles*, Hounslow Language Centre)

5f

SHAKI

This is my language autobiography and it starts when I was under 3 weeks old.

I was born in Nigeria so my first words reflect the country I was living in. But needless to say I underwent the same process of language identity as other babies.

This process started with gurgling noises which became 'words' like aaa ohoh and da. In our house there was always a lot of people so a lot of speech was used. Because I was the only baby in the house I was encouraged at an early age to imitate speech. When I was about eight months old I was stringing two words together like: Shakira alero which means Shaki have.

I was about five years old when we moved to London so my 1000 words of Yoruba (Nigerian dialect) where useless. But it didn't take too long to learn the necessary English words to be just understood. Learning English became much easier when I started school.

When I go back to Nigeria I find myself talking in pidgin English and saying things like: 'Wettin you'd be doing?' meaning 'What are you doing?' I do this because it gives me an excuse to be

lazy with my English, and also so my Nigerian relatives can understand me.
(*Language Profiles*, Hounslow Language Centre)

Whatever else, the reflections in the above language autobiographies offer powerful illustrations of the awareness students have of English language forms.

A group of 7- to 8-year-old children in a school in Derbyshire, England, were recently involved in investigating aspects of Earth in relation to the solar system. As an introduction to the topic, the teacher introduced them to a book (Cole and Degen 1990) which presented aspects of space exploration from three different perspectives:

1. A story about a space journey;
2. Information about the planets and the solar system;
3. 'Comic-style' speech from the main characters.

It was the children's task to create their own book about 'space', using the three forms of the original text: narrative, information, speech bubbles. The opportunity to create texts in three different styles allowed the children to compare and contrast the different forms used, and this, naturally led to a discussion of what makes each form distinctive.

NARRATIVE

5g
The bus arrived at the school. The children got their coats on and climbed on to the bus. The teacher, Miss Lilly, counted everyone on and the children rushed to find a seat. Charlotte was eating her crisps. Somebody pushed her and they went all over the floor.
(Author's data)

Many of the children's original versions were written in the present tense: *arrives*, *get*, *climb* etc, and this allowed the teacher the opportunity to discuss with the children the difference this made:

Helen: with <u>arrives</u> it's as if it's happening now – it's just a bit
      more exciting
Julie: <u>arrived</u> means it's already happened – it happened before

On the basis of these observations, the children then selected the style they felt most appropriate for their own 'books'.

INFORMATION

5h

Granada Studios Present
JOURNEY TO
THE PLANETS
An exciting, realistic adventure. It takes you to
Venus, Mercury and the Milky Way.
Be brought into the journey.
ON NOW!

(Author's data)

This advert for the film showing at the studio which is the school bus's destination is part of the same double-page format. Here the children were involved in incorporating information in the format of a persuasive poster. In this situation, discussion focused on <u>audience</u>:
— keep it short
— use big letters and exclamation marks
— get them interested
— 'it's like you're talking to people'.

Again, the emphasis was specifically on discussing words or expressions appropriate for particular situations.

SPEECH BUBBLES

Here, the commentary produced by the children was much more concerned with the use of colloquial, informal, even non-Standard, utterances:

51
— *this is brill . . . I like this film*
— *it's not boring . . . it's cool dude*
— *don't show off*
— *brillo*
— *I don't believe in space*
— *this is fab*
(Author's data)

In particular, it was the use of specific vocabulary items that was commented upon – words in current favour for use in informal contexts: *brill, cool dude, fab* etc. This can also provide an opportunity to consider the words that are constantly entering, and then leaving, the English language.

blip:	*brief set-back in a particular trend*
couch potato:	*lazy TV-watching person*
hands-on:	*directly involved at a practical level*
mega:	*great in importance, quality or size*
wannabe:	*dedicated follower*

All are words that enter the language, sometimes through advertising, but also through teenage culture.

Such case-studies as the foregoing emphasize the importance of creating situations where children and older students can 'talk about texts' and about the flexibility and immense variety of the English language.

Let us create a Standard – or better still, let us create standards which command our assent because we understand how and why they have come into being and because we realize that they are not immutable laws but conventions of human behaviour, subject to time and change. And let us never again be afraid of splitting our infinitives, fusing our participles, or even of not knowing when to use the Present Perfect Continuous, for a standard is one thing and stuff is another. (Nash 1992: 14)

Being knowledgeable about language and being proficient in its use are inextricably linked; and both of these goals need to inform any study of Standard and non-Standard forms of the language.

5.6 The development aspect of KAL (Knowledge About Language)

The National Curriculum in England and Wales is based on a developmental model of language use, yet it is difficult to discuss KAL within this framework. The levels and extent of KAL teaching increase dramatically at Key Stages 3 and 4, causing teachers at Key Stages 1 and 2 to query why such aspects of language study should only begin to occur at secondary level.

A simplistic approach would be, for example, to say that the developmental process is one, throughout the school years, of gradually making implicit knowledge about language explicit; or to say that some topics (such as speech/writing differences) are more suitable areas of study for younger or older children. But, as several teachers have realized, knowledge about language does not lend itself to being categorized or pigeon-holed in this way. As many schools have now observed, and as we have seen above, a possible 'way forward' in terms of development is to build into a school's language policies situations in the classroom where teachers can, over the years, create contexts for children both to <u>collect</u> examples of language use and also to <u>compare</u> and <u>classify</u> it in some way. The analysis then leads to an increased 'making sense' of what the language does.

In primary and secondary schools involved in creating KAL contexts in the classroom, it has become evident that children come to school already in possession of an extensive implicit knowledge about language. For example, many will have read signs used for different purposes, will have seen writing used in diverse contexts, and will have heard talk used for a variety of reasons. A language policy which acknowledges, and makes use of, this implicit awareness can help children from the early stages of their development to become effective language users.

SUMMARY

- There is a need for schools to develop in their students a greater awareness of how language works, based on the assumption of a connection between pupils' ability to discuss texts explicitly and their capacity to produce effective spoken and written English.
- Any study of Standard English (both spoken and written) needs to be seen in the context of the situations in which spoken and written language actually occurs.
- Students need to be provided with a framework for investigating language in its context – in this case, a collect–compare–classify approach.
- It has become evident that children come to school already in possession of an extensive implicit knowledge about language.

6 Assessing Standard English

We need to look at the productive skills of speakers (and writers) in terms of a strategic accomplishment in performance and not in terms of a deficit or inadequacy in competence. It is impossible to define what constitutes the minimal competence one must have to be adequate except relative to the norms of a particular community . . . It will mean at the same time recognizing students' rights to their own language.

S. Romaine, *The Language of Children and Adolescents*

In a previous chapter differences and distinctions between written and spoken language were explored, with particular reference to Standard English. The complexities raised by the question of what precisely constitutes the standard are especially pertinent at the interface of spoken and written forms. In this chapter we continue to explore spoken and written language, but from the perspective of children's language development. The main focus for the chapter is on the need to assess children's language development in a fair and balanced way. Assessment is a necessary component in a teaching programme, but it should be used as supportively as possible and, in the case of language development, must recognize the kinds of complexity concerning Standard English discussed in the previous chapters.

6.1 Sampling and analysing

ACTIVITY

With particular reference to the discussion in chapter 4, analyse the following samples of children's speech and writing. Highlight the positive features of language use in each case, and isolate those aspects which, with the support of the teacher, require further development.

6a

(Ian: oral narrative)

when I was ... when I was ... I lived down old end and I was only about four or five and erm I was on this little motor bike thing and er ... yer know one o' these small uns and I had a big pencil in mi mouth yer know one o' the big thick ones and erm I fell off the mo ... I fell off it and it was in mi mouth and the ... and it ... it it hit the floor and it went straight into mi gum up the top and the ... and it nearly went down mi mouth and I could have choked but it ... it just hit the gum ... anyway I went to hospital and I ... when I come back out I had a big hole in mi gum

(Author's data)

Here, Ian (an 11-year-old boy), is relating to a group of peers an incident that happened to him when he was younger. He has already listened to two others in the group telling of accidents that happened to them when they were young; so, one of his main aims in telling the story is, in some sense, to 'top' what he has just heard.

It is generally thought that speech is often non-Standard (in the sense of being ungrammatical), as, for example, in the form *when I <u>come</u> back out* instead of *when I <u>came</u> back out*. It may, therefore, be useful to establish the grammatical bases in Ian's narrative.

In line 1 there is a false start with an adverbial time clause *when I was*. This is repeated and then rejected. In its grammatical structure, however, it is perfectly regular. The rest of the clause/sentence structures, though simple, are also regular; for example:

Subject	Verb	Object	Adverbial phrase
I	*lived*		
I	*was*		*on this little motor bike thing*
I	*fell off*	*it*	

In those places where there may be a sense of ungrammaticalness, it is not to do with syntactic problems but with interruptions or, typically in this text, additional information tacked on in loosely appositional structures, as in: *. . . yer know one o' these small uns/. . . yer know one o' the big thick ones.*

Thus, while speech is likely to be less tightly structured than writing, it is clearly not ungrammatical. The looser structuring derives, in the main, from the manner in which additional information can be added as an afterthought. This often provides structures that seem unlike written structures. They none the less conform to the same patterns. We need, then, to distinguish between structures that are commonly found in informal speech and those required in writing; we need also to distinguish between ungrammatical structures/usages and dialect forms, such as *when I come back out*.

An assessment of Ian's narrative would need to clear up these potential misconceptions and focus, instead, on its communicative impact. In this respect, it is clear that he is able to manipulate the basic incident to achieve maximum effect. He makes the motor bike *little . . . yer know one o' these small uns*, but the pencil *big . . . yer know one o' the big thick ones*. He also uses exaggeration effectively to make the details of the injury suitably shocking.

6b

(group discussion: sewage)

Anne: *well, first of all, we'd to have the streams drained out and cleaned . . . and um . . . we'd have to have better toilets than what there were already*

Beverley: *while the drainage were going on I think . . . they er they should . . . make . . . new drainlines so that they should go . . . so the sewage should go to the places instead of back in the stream and then they would . . . and if it went back in the stream again with it being . . . drained out I think they . . . they'd get typhoid again wouldn't they . . . so . . . they'd have to make a new drainage*

Carol: *I think they should've made little wooden bins to clip on the end of the wood and then . . . every day they should take it out and empty it somewhere convenient and if it would they could burn it*

Beverley: *er I think that's quite a good idea and . . . erm . . . they'd have to tell the people first . . . about how they're catching this disease . . . and erm*

Carol: *but would the people understand because they're only common people and not educational jobs or anything*

Anne: *I know but they could explain it in a . . . in a simplified yeah manner*

Carol: *I don't think they'd listen to you*

Beverley: *ah but would . . . would erm would they believe you when they said they were contact . . . contract . . . contracting it from the stream*

Anne: *well they'd probably would believe you after they'd been seen all these people with the disease they'd have to listen they'd have to be aware of getting this disease so they must listen*

(Author's data)

In this extract a group of three students (Year 10) is investigating
the causes of the spread of typhoid fever using some original
source materials. The problem set by their teacher is for them to
discuss how the spread of infection might have best been
prevented.

All three students have recognizable northern accents and
there are some examples of non-Standard forms of English: *than
what there were already* / *While the drainage were going on*. Because of the informal nature of the conversation, there is a high
incidence of interrupted, repeated and revised structures: *well
they'd probably would* / *I think they they'd get typhoid* / *and if it
would they could burn it*. Often, because of this, speech of this
kind is considered to be ungrammatical, when in fact such
features are typical of speech that is exploratory, tentative and
reflective. The informality of the situation is also shown in their
constant use of repetitions – *they er they should* / *would erm
would they* / *they'd have to . . . they'd have to* – and in the changes
made to grammatical structure: *and not educational jobs or
anything*.

In spite of the informality, however, some of the clause
structures are quite complex. For example, Beverley's first contri-
bution has a series of main clauses linked by the conjunct *so*,
which she uses to make general inferences from her observations.
Subordinate clauses qualify and clarify such inferences: *While
the drainage were going on . . .* / *if it went back in the stream again
. . .* Each girl picks up, and reflects on, previous remarks, as
evidenced in the repeated verb structures which they use: *have to
have, I think they, they'd have to*. Also, the modality of a lot of
what they have to say illustrates the tentative nature of their
discussion and their willingness to explore each other's ideas:
should, could, would, probably.

It is largely acknowledged that, in spite of the differences,
there is, grammatically and lexically, a large area of common ground between Standard and non-Standard English; and

speakers of English will not necessarily use either consistently, but will vary according to <u>situation</u> and <u>purpose</u>. It might be argued that, in talk, the more formal the situation, the more likely a speaker is to use Standard forms of the language. But even in this fairly informal group discussion between friends, there are few examples of non-Standard forms.

Any assessment, then, needs to take the above points into account and to focus, crucially, on the following questions:

— how far have the pupils achieved their purpose?
— how effectively do they collaborate in finding solutions to the given problem?
— how regularly do they stay 'on task'?

6c

(Geoffrey: written diary)

My school is horrid they give you roten milk and I can tell you how Rotten the milk is in class 5 I cold not drink all my milk, cos it is so rotten so I dissided to make a plan my teacher was away and the class was took over by Miss Marliedn and I cold not drink it fast becous it was so rotten and when the class went out to play I empted the cartin milk into the sink and I went out to play and Jimmy Bennet was surprised to see me at play but I dident mind cous God had mad me very glad but now Ime in class two I've got good at Drinking Milk But there was a nuvver probblem sums so I got a nuvver plan in my head and do you know what it was to cheat I counted in ones By putting ones all up my book untill I had 16 and that was what the number was at the top of my page so that was a nuvver problem dilld with but there was a nuvver probblem what no one cold get rod of But I cold that was writeting so I got near a boy with chicken pocks so I could not go to school.
(Author's data)

Geoffrey's vividly dramatic diary account of days in his school life, like Ian's narrative, owes much of its liveliness to the inclusion of features typical in speech. There are some examples of non-Standard grammatical forms – *the class was* <u>*took over*</u> (taken over), <u>*what*</u> *no one cold get rod of* (that) – but the main features of Geoffrey's writing reflect those that are more frequently found in speech, such as the frequent use of *and* as a linking word. Others, however, are closer to a <u>writerly</u> style, for example the use of a non-finite subordinate clause which is <u>almost</u> right: *By putting ones all up my book* (Geoffrey has not, however, clearly linked it to a main clause).

Geoffrey assumes a reader shares the same 'personal' world that he does – that his reader knows, for instance, who *Jimmy Bennet* and *Miss Marliedn* are, without needing any explanation. He also writes in an anecdotal way. Several of his expressions are like remarks addressed to a listener: *do you know what it was to cheat*. He asks a direct question, using the personal pronoun *you*; and the whole sentence has the tone of something that is spoken rather than written.

Geoffrey's 'speaking' voice makes the writing very vivid, lively and personal; but the reader is left to do a lot of guesswork. Obviously the teacher is in a very good position to be able to do this, because s/he knows Geoffrey and his 'world' – the world of class and playground. But this very fact might well lead the teacher to overestimate Geoffrey's ability to communicate effectively. This ability is obviously more than simply being able to write in Standard English; it means being able to develop a <u>writerly</u> style which will enable him to communicate successfully with a wider range of audiences than simply those that share his common assumptions.

6d

(David: written account)

A PILOT IN HOSPITAL HIDING

One day in Would warr II there was a airrade warning so some of the British planes went up but arfer a while some of the planes got

shot down. The man had broken his arm and leg. He heard the Jermans coming and had to take cover by now it was night. Soon the Jermans would be out scaning the area. He had to hide. He needed aid quick then he heard a pack of English men coming. he called help help they come to get him and then they went to take him to camp hospital but the jermans starrted fireing at them but the english over came them and they took him to hospital
(Author's data)

Eleven-year-old David has here produced a story of an incident set in the Second World War. The only non-Standard forms to be found are: *He needed aid quick* and they *come to get him*. In the second instance it is possible to argue that, because this text was a 'one-off' piece of writing, the form might well have arisen as a change of tense from past to present, where David unintentionally moves from recollection to actuality – a frequent feature of young writers and their stories. The entire text consists, grammatically, of simple main clauses, some of which are linked with *so*, *and* and *but*. Where there is potential confusion in the grammatical and lexical organization of the text, however, is in David's use of 'vague' subject references: *some of the British planes, The man, the Jermans, He, they, the jermans, the english*. At times, this makes it difficult for the reader to establish what is happening, who is doing what to whom, and where it is all taking place.

Clearly, non-Standard forms of English, where David uses them, do not cause serious comprehension problems. Some difficulties, therefore, are purely on the surface. They might upset some people, but they do not, usually, inhibit genuine communication. In David's case, communication is more likely to be impaired when the grammatical links he makes, in stringing his ideas together, do not have precise enough points of reference (although most of the forms used are Standard English).

6e

(Lesley: written report)

A DEAD PIDGIN

To day at afternoon play just when we was comeing back in to school Mrs B found a pidgin on the floor next to the Haygreen Lane side. Some children had gone in but I was ther when Gary Destains said hay up thers a pidgin on floor. We all rusht up and Mrs B showted 'stop come back and let me look whats apend to it poor thing.' I just thout it was resting a bit but Dobbie said its ded it was when Mrs B picket it up its kneck just flopped over poor thing I said to Dobbie. She lifted it up with its wings and they were like big lovely grey fans. I didn't know wings were so lovely and big with so meny fethers espeshily When we had gon in we was just sittind in are class and telling Mrs Sandison and the others about it when Mrs B came and held it up with its lovely grey wings I was sorry for it poor thing and Mrs Sandison was sad and we all was.

(Author's data)

Ten-year-old Lesley's writing contains the following features of, and influences from, the variety of English widely used in South Yorkshire:

1. *we <u>was</u> comeing*	(SE: *we <u>were</u> coming*)
we <u>was</u> just sittind	(SE: *we <u>were</u> just sitting*)
we all <u>was</u>	(SE: *we all <u>were</u>*)
2. *hay up*	no automatic equivalent in SE; approximates to 'now then' or 'what's this?' depending on context.
3. *whats <u>a</u>pend*	(SE: *what happened?*) aspirated <u>h</u> at the beginning of words is uncommon in South Yorkshire speech and Leslie transcribes the word as it is spoken.

4. *ther* and *thers*   Again, the words are transcribed here as they are spoken.

5. *on floor*   We can see the influence of the elision of <u>the</u>, the definite article, in some contexts in South Yorkshire speech.

On the basis of one piece of writing it is, of course, difficult to know at what stage of development Lesley is; to standardize her writing in places may therefore be counter-productive, and may only serve to discourage her from her individual shaping of the narrative. In general, however, it is worth distinguishing two main phases in her writing: a <u>spoken</u> report (highlighting what was said) and a <u>written</u> report (highlighting what was done and what actions were taken). In the case of the former, non-Standard forms are quite appropriate and, in fact, add both immediacy and a local character to the main actors in the narrative; in the case of the latter, Standard forms would be more appropriate. Thus, *we was comeing back* in the first line would be appropriate dialogue, but it is not appropriate as written narrative report; while *Hay up* and *whats apend* may remain as part of the narrative dialogue and cannot really be corrected, since there is no agreed way in which spoken dialect forms are represented in Standard written spelling.

Lesley's story provides a good example of a pupil's knowledge about language, particularly of distinctions between Standard and non-Standard forms in written and spoken contexts, being developed from their own production of language. (Chapter 5 gives particular guidance on appropriate methodologies for developing greater knowledge about language.) For a fuller discussion of Lesley's writing as well as other similar examples, see also Harris (1993) – a book in the same series as this one – especially chapter 5.

6.2 Developmental aspects of Standard English

In the use of Standard English there is a clear developmental aspect. This has to do with a growing appreciation of the need for formal language and also a growing control over specific registers. The following examples from Richards (1978) illustrate these two points. The examples are <u>typical</u> responses to a request to describe an earthworm, in writing.

At age 7+   *It is brown, wiggly, it's long.*

At age 10+   *It is long and thin. It is brown in colour. It has rings round it. It has no eyes. It is slimy.*

At age 12+   *It is long and thin and brown. It has segments along its body. It has a black patch on it called a saddle. Its skin has rough patches underneath. It is slimy.*

At age 14+   *It is long thin and brownish in colour. Has segments running along it. Front end is circular and pointed. Back end broad and flattish. Has a broad segment nearer the front end called the saddle. It has small hairs under its body. It is covered with slime. It has a line down its body which is a vein, running from top to bottom.*

At age 16+   *The earthworm has a body shaped like a closed tube made up of segments or rings which help to make it flexible. The mouth of the animal is at the pointed end – the anus at the flattened end. There is a blood vessel running down the dorsal surface of the animal and visible through the skin. Approximately one third of the body length from the mouth end is the saddle which is unsegmented. All the body is moist to touch.*

These representative examples underline that the acquisition of appropriate writerly forms and of the Standard English forms which normally accompany them is part of a developmental process. If the teacher intervenes too early or too inflexibly to 'correct' inappropriate forms, then there are dangers that this process of development may be impaired, not least because the confidence of the writer can be affected; as a result, attention to linguistic form may obstruct what the writer actually wants to say. On the other hand, if teachers adopt too flexible an approach and fail to develop their pupils' knowledge about language, especially knowledge about differences between speech and writing and the appropriate functions of Standard and non-Standard language, then what the writer wants to say may always lack an appropriate form and the pupil's acquisition of Standard Englishes may fail to be achieved.

SUMMARY

- Development of Standard forms should be seen as part of a growing understanding of the handling of more formal aspects of language use.
- Standard/non-Standard forms in children's language production need to be considered alongside other aspects of language use.

7 Conclusion

7a

Heard the One about the Bloke
Who Tried to Dodge His Road Tax.
He Got Hit with a £1000 Fine.
  GET IT
(Advert on the back of a bus, December 1993)

7b

Dear Mrs P
Daniel was off school on Friday because he did not feel like
coming so he said bugger it, I'll have a day off.
(Parent, Year 7 pupil, Yorkshire school)

It is impossible to deny the versatility of the English language.
Many effective instances of English contain mixtures of different
styles, ranging from the formal to the informal, whether it be an
advert for public display or a quick note scribbled to a class
teacher. In contrast with these informal texts, 'so-called' Standard English can often cause comprehension difficulties.

ACTIVITY

Read through the following texts and consider some of the
difficulties they may present to a reader. Offer 'alternative' ways
of writing the texts.

7c

In consequence of the non-payment of the above-noted account
and your failure to avail yourself of the facilities afforded to you

in our reminder notice already sent to you, an employee of the Board will call at your premises for the purpose of obtaining a meter reading and disconnecting the supply on the 10th March.
(Letter from the electricity board to a customer)

7d

The Council is faced with the mammoth task of disposing of this rubbish – rubbish generated by industry and the $2\frac{3}{4}$ million residents of the County along with massive amounts of civic amenities (bulky household items and material delivered to disposal sites, etc., by the general public), trade and other refuse created within the area.
(Council leaflet on the siting of a tip)

7e

You are advised that any drain land before 1st October, 1937 serving more than one property is, under SS/20/24 of the Public Health Act, 1936, a sewer vested in the council (who, in the event of failure of owners to carry out the necessary work, become responsible for the maintenance and repair, rechargeable to the owners affected), and before such a sewer can be built over an agreement (under S.25 PHA 1936) to safeguard the council's right of access to the sewer must be entered into by the property owner.
(Council letter to a resident)

(Plain English Campaign 1986)

Clearly (or unclearly), texts produced in Standard English can create their own problems both grammatically and lexically.

In text **7c**, the opening sentence from an electricity board's letter to a customer is 55 words long, but, because of its grammatical complexity, it is difficult to disentangle the meaning. The 'underlying' points are:
— you haven't paid the bill;
— you didn't contact us to use one of the payment methods shown on the reminder;

— we are coming to cut off your electricity.

More effective versions might help the reader to see the <u>structure</u> of what is being said more clearly.

Again, in text **7d**, the writer is essentially trying to make two 'underlying' points:

— this will be a big job;
— the rubbish, of different types, comes from industry, commerce and residents.

A more successful text would, perhaps, result from a more informal style, where the structures used take account of the reader's personal circumstances and are more interactive: *Where does all this rubbish come from? It's produced by <u>every</u> industry.* Such an approach might well utilize, as here, some of the features more associated with speech.

Similarly, text **7e** has specific points to make:

— the council has certain rights and duties concerning sewers;
— the council's right of access needs protecting.

Here, the legal requirement of mentioning Acts of Parliament gets in the way of our understanding of the text.

Standard English, therefore, can be seen as containing many varieties, which overlap and change according to the nature and audience of the situation. It is a flexible, and constantly changing, vehicle.

Excessive formality in English usage must not be confused with 'Standard English'; a text can be informal and Standard, and communicate effectively, while a more formal text, also Standard, can be difficult to understand.

The essential point is that a standard English, like other varieties of language, develops endo-normatively, by a continuing process of self-regulation, as appropriate to different conditions of use. It is not fixed, therefore, by native speakers. They have no special say in the matter, in spite of their claims to ownership of real English as associated with their own particular cultural contexts of use. (Widdowson 1993, page 8)

Further reading

Bain, R., B. Fitzgerald and **M. Taylor** (eds.). 1992. *Looking into Language – Classroom Approaches to Knowledge About Language*. London: Hodder and Stoughton.

This practical, classroom-based book illustrates a range of activities for exploring and investigating uses of language at primary and secondary levels. The focus is upon the development of knowledge about language across the curriculum, and the book presents a series of case-studies which explore attempts to foster children's understanding of the nature of language use. Specific chapters focus on speech/writing differences and on the nature of language diversity.

Cox, B. 1991. *Cox on Cox – an English Curriculum for the 1990s*. London: Hodder and Stoughton.

In May 1989, the National Curriculum English Working Group submitted its final recommendations on English teaching in England and Wales. This report, *English for ages 5 to 16*, was produced under the chairmanship of Brian Cox, and this book provides a useful commentary on its creation. Whilst providing the teacher with insightful comments on all aspects of the English curriculum, it has a particularly revealing chapter on Standard English which outlines the Committee's observations on this topic, alongside the political machinations that they had to contend with.

Crowley, T. 1989. *The Politics of Discourse*. London: Macmillan.

This book introduces the reader to many accounts of the study of language in Britain over the past century and a half, evaluating such studies in the context of their political and cultural influences. Again, the notion of 'standard' language or languages looms prominently and the current 'English' debate is set clearly in the context of its historical evolution.

Fairclough, N. 1989. *Language and Power*. London: Longman.

This book presents a fascinating and lively account of how language functions in the maintaining and changing of power relations, showing how, in analysing such language uses, we can become more conscious of them, and help to resist, or even change, them. It includes several insightful observations on the nature of 'standardization', but, above all, it offers an approach to linguistic investigation that is a 'model' for much of the practical work on aspects of Standard English that are explored in this book.

Fairclough, N. (ed.). 1992. *Critical Language Awareness*. London: Longman.

This book contains many suggestions for helping pupils and teachers to observe and reflect upon language from a more critical perspective. It consists of a collection of articles which draw attention to the structure and functions of language in relation to language in education. Notions of 'standards' in language are explored in 'The appropriacy of "appropriateness"'; and there are useful investigations into the development of 'language awareness' as a means of promoting effective language skills.

Halliday, M. A. K. 1989. *Spoken and Written Language*. Oxford: Oxford University Press.

This book provides a comprehensive and readable guide to the differences and similarities between speech and writing. It takes us from the development of speech in infancy, through an account of the writing systems, to a comparative treatment of spoken and written language. Speech emerges as no less important than writing; the two serve different goals.

Harris, J. and J. Wilkinson (eds.). 1990. *In the Know – a Guide to English Language in the National Curriculum*. Cheltenham: Stanley Thornes.

A collection of articles introducing aspects of English in the National Curriculum. Whilst covering the more 'traditional' aspects of English teaching, it also considers features of language teaching such as Standard English and knowledge about language. Its main emphasis is on exploring the relationship between language awareness and language production.

McArthur, T. (ed.). 1992. *The Oxford Companion to the English Language*. Oxford: Oxford University Press.

This is certainly a large and impressive language reference book. As well as including detailed, yet succinct, entries on major aspects of English usage (such as grammar, spelling, pronunciation etc), it has many thought-provoking comments to make on standards of English and Standard English. In particular, it looks at these in both national and international contexts.

Milroy, J. and L. Milroy. 1991. *Authority in Language – Investigating Language Prescription and Standardization*. London: Routledge.

The book examines clearly and creatively prescriptive judgements about language use, and the effects that such evaluations have both on society and on the individuals that use the language. It covers many aspects: the role of standardization; the historical development of the English language; differences in speech and writing; concepts of 'grammaticality' and 'acceptability'; and the relationship between language prescription and teaching. Clear in its evaluation of many research findings, it provides a useful discussion of the 'good English' debate.

Mittins, W. 1991. *Language Awareness for Teachers*. Milton Keynes: Open University Press.

This book provides an informative, linguistically driven introduction for teachers to the teaching of English language within the context of the National Curriculum. It explores aspects of language study relevant to the classroom situation and covers many topics that have a bearing on the Standard/non-Standard debate. Overall, this is a very approachable book on a range of language issues.

Nash, W. 1992. *An Uncommon Tongue – the Uses and Resources of English*. London: Routledge.

This book contains helpful reflections on the nature of language and, supported by a variety of examples, looks at the 'merits' of both descriptive and prescriptive approaches to language study. In particular, it raises questions about 'Standard English' in its early chapters on 'Standards and stuff' and 'Usage, users and the used'.

Phillipson, R. 1992. *Linguistic Imperialism*. Oxford: Oxford University Press.

This text explores the contemporary nature of English as a world language, and sets out to discover, initially, how the language became so dominant and why. As Phillipson argues: 'The British empire has given way to the empire of English.' By relating linguistic description to the social sciences, he tries to illustrate the nature of linguistic imperialism (both past and present) in relation to English language teaching.

Quirk, R. and **G. Stein**. 1990. *English in Use*. London: Longman.

Very much a guide to the varieties of English currently in use, this book contains some useful accounts of notions of Standard English in both national and international contexts. In particular, each chapter has practical 'follow-up' activities that can be used to explore the nature of language in context.

Stubbs, M. 1988. *Educational Linguistics*. Oxford: Basil Blackwell.

This book offers many insights into the relationship between linguistics and English in education. It deals thoughtfully and comprehensively with aspects of both spoken and written English; and, in particular, contains a well-argued section on the teaching of spoken and written Standard English in schools.

Todd, L. and **I. Hancock**. 1990. *International English Usage*. London: Routledge.

This is a very comprehensive guide to both spoken and written English in its detailed exploration of language usage in all the countries where English is widely used. The authors state their two goals clearly: to deal objectively with English as a worldwide language with many local varities; to distinguish legitimate regional practices from actual errors. Above all, the book acknowledges the diversity of the English language, and looks at the English language as it is, rather than as some tell us it should be.

Glossary

accent Accent describes those features of the pronunciation of a language which identify a person either geographically or socially. A geographical accent is associated with a specific town or city (for example, Liverpool, Birmingham, Bristol), or a particular region (for example, the Black Country, the Fens), or with national groups speaking the same language (for example, Australian, American).

Social accents are more the result of a person's social and educational background. An example of this in Britain is Received Pronunciation (RP), commonly known as 'BBC English', 'posh' or 'Oxford English'. This is an accent which, from a geographical point of view, is neutral (that is, it has no regional associations), although it is often associated with public schools and professional uses. Because of its 'now' non-regional associations, speaking in RP is regarded (wrongly) as speaking with no accent at all. In terms of linguistic description, everyone speaks with an accent, varying according to geographical, social or individual situations.

dialect Dialect refers to the varieties of language that can be identified either geographically or socially by the use of distinctive **grammatical** or vocabulary features (for example, *Her's saft* is a West Midlands expression, consisting of the grammatical use of *her* where **Standard** English would use *she*, and where the word *saft* is a dialectal combination of Standard English vocabulary terms *soft* and *daft*. **Spoken** forms of a dialect often become associated with a distinctively recognizable pronunciation (an **accent**). The 'dialect' that now predominates in English (especially in writing) is called Standard English.

grammar In most traditions of linguistic description, grammar is seen as one of the three components of language structure – the other two are phonology and semantics. Grammar is also usually limited to the analysis of structures at and below sentence **level** (in terms of its **syntax, morphology** or both). A distinction is often made between descriptive grammar and prescriptive grammar. A descriptive approach aims to give as precise an account of the grammar of a language in terms of the rules for actual **usage** at a particular point of time in its existence. A prescriptive approach sets down certain rules for usage, stating what should, or should not, occur. The descriptive and evaluative aspects of these approaches significantly highlight the current debate as to what constitutes 'good' and 'bad' English and they are very much of relevance in trying to establish the precise nature of what constitutes **Spoken Standard** and **Written** Standard English.

KAL   KAL is a term now much used in discussions of the teaching of English as a mother tongue. It stands for Knowledge About Language, whereby, in accordance with the National Curriculum for English in England and Wales, pupils are introduced to a systematic study of the structure and functions of the English language. It is argued that highlighting aspects of language use in this way may well help pupils and students to enrich their own experiences of **speaking** and listening, reading and **writing**. The emphasis, however, is on developing new exploratory and investigative approaches to language rather than on the decontextualized teaching of parts of speech inherited from language teaching in the 1950s. Its focus is not exclusively on the **grammatical** features of language but also, for example, on semantic and **contextual** features. (See Bain, R., B. Fitzgerald and M. Taylor (eds.) 1992)

language awareness   This is a term generally used in modern foreign language teaching and to a lesser extent in EFL/ESL teaching to refer to an approach to teaching which, during the process of language learning, draws attention to aspects of the nature and functions of language. Proponents of greater language awareness (as with those who teach **KAL**) argue that more explicit and conscious attention to the systematic organization of language is a prerequisite for success in language learning (See Mittins, W. 1991)

language change   This refers to the modification of the forms of the language over a period of time. In linguistic study two broad perspectives of variation are commonly identified. One is variation over time (diachronic); and this takes into account the changes that have occurred historically between, say, Old, Middle and Modern English. The other broad perspective is of synchronic variation, which accounts for aspects of variety at a given point in time and is almost always used to indicate a study of language use contemporary with the writer (or speaker). (See Phillipson, R. 1992)

lexis   Vocabulary, or lexis, is often regarded in language teaching as a limited range of words that progresses to a more extended range. There is obviously a partial truth in this viewpoint; but it is sometimes inevitably also associated with the notion that some words are intrinsically better than others: how many teachers of English, for instance, universally condemn the use of the word *nice*. This idea of 'good' words needs to be considered critically, since words, in isolation, can never be deemed good, bad or indifferent. Vocabulary has a multiplicity of functions dependent on **context** and use. Words are obviously single items; but in partnership with other words they perform lexical and grammatical functions; and recent studies have demonstrated the important role that vocabulary plays in the formation of complete **spoken** and **written texts**. (See Nash, W. 1992)

spoken and written language   Speaking and writing are two major modes of language organization and need to be seen as alternative but 'equal' systems of linguistic expression. In their extreme forms, for example, a casual conversation between friends and a formal business letter, there are a number of significant linguistic differences. For example, some **grammatical** constructions are found more frequently in writing (for example, passive verbal phrases: *it was decided*); and certain items of vocabulary rarely, or never, occur in writing (for example, the expression used, in English, to identify that the speaker has forgotten, or does not know, the name of the item: *whatchamacallit*). Also, speech is dynamic and transient; whereas writing is static and permanent. However, spoken and written language are best seen as sets of tendencies; and there are, of course, many examples, such as much contemporary advertising copy, of one category overlapping into another. (See Halliday, M. A. K. 1989)

Glossary

standard and non-standard   Standard is the term that is frequently used to refer to a form of the language which has considerable prestige and is considered to be a uniform variety of a language; whereas non-standard tends to be associated with **dialects**, colloquial **usage** and slang. The actual situation is, in fact, much more complex than this oversimplified binary division suggests. Language is inevitably much more complex and variable than this simplistic labelling suggests. (See Milroy, J. and L. Milroy 1991)

text   This is a term commonly used by linguists to refer to any 'stretch' of language (either spoken or written) that has been collected for the purpose of analysis and description (for example, examples of **Standard** English used in conversational exchanges or pieces of children's writing that begin to employ Standard English forms). Any text, therefore, is seen as having a specific purpose in a specific **context**. It is seen essentially as a complete semantic unit and does not consist of isolated words and sentences. This concept is particularly useful when exploring the Standard English debate, for it assumes that the judgement of the validity of any text (be it one word, one phrase or a continuous series of utterances) has to be in terms of its context.

References

Achebe, C. 1965. English and the African writer. *Transition*, 1, 2.

Adams, M. J. 1990. *Beginning to Read*. London: MIT Press.

Bradbury, M. 1983. *Rates of Exchange*. London: Secker and Warburg.

Brautigan, R. 1971. *Revenge of the Lawn*. New York: Simon and Schuster.

Carter, R. (ed.). 1990. *Knowledge about Language and the Curriculum*. London: Hodder and Stoughton.

Cole, J. and B. Degen. 1990. *The Magic Bus – Lost in the Solar System*. London: Kingfisher Books.

Cox, B. 1989. *English teaching – the need for reform, or the new curriculum*. Collins English Dictionary Annual Lecture, Glasgow.

Cox, B. 1991. *Cox on Cox – an English Curriculum for the 1990s*. London: Hodder and Stoughton.

DES. 1989. *Report of the English Working Party 5–16 – the Cox Report*. London: HMSO.

Donmall, G. (ed.). 1985. *Language Awareness*. London: CILT.

Ede, J. and J. Williamson. 1980. *Talking, Listening and Learning*. London: Longman.

Edwards, V. 1984. *Language Variation in the Multicultural Classroom*. Reading: Centre for the Teaching of Reading.

Ellis, G. and B. Sinclair. 1989. *Learning How to Learn English*. Cambridge: Cambridge University Press.

Ezekiel, N. 1982. The Patriot. In *Latter Day Psalms*. Oxford: Oxford University Press.

Giles, H. and H. Powesland. 1975. *Speech and Social Evaluation*. London: Academic Press.

Harris, J. 1993. *Introducing Writing*. London: Penguin.

Leith, D. 1983. *A Social History of English*. London: Routledge.

Lutrario, C. 1993. *Exploring Language*. Aylesbury: Ginn.

References

McArthur, T. (ed.). 1992. *The Oxford Companion to the English Language*. Oxford: Oxford University Press.

McCabe, C. 1990. Language, literature, identity – reflections on the Cox Report. *Critical Quarterly*, 32, 4.

McCarthy, M. and **R. Carter.** 1994. *Language as Discourse – Perspectives for Language Teaching*. Harlow: Longman.

Marenbon, J. 1987. *English Our English – the New Orthodoxy Examined*. London: Centre for Policy Studies.

Milroy, J. and **L. Milroy.** 1991. *Authority in Language – Investigating Language Prescription and Standardization*. London: Routledge.

Nash, W. 1992. *An Uncommon Tongue – the Uses and Resources of English*. London: Routledge.

Oxford Reference Dictionary. 1984. Quoted in Romaine 1984.

Perera, K. 1987. *Understanding Language*. Pamphlet of the NAAE (National Association of Advisers in English): Sheffield.

Pinter, H. 1991. *Plays: Four*. London: Faber and Faber.

Platt, J., H. Weber and **M. L. Ho.** 1984. *The New Englishes*. London: Routledge.

Research Machines plc. 1992. *User Guide to NB300 Research Machine*. Oxford: Research Machines plc.

Richards, J. 1978. *Classroom Language*. London: Allen and Unwin.

Romaine, S. 1984. *The Language of Children and Adolescents – the Acquisition of Communicative Competence*. Oxford: Basil Blackwell.

Stubbs, M. 1988. *Educational Linguistics*. Oxford: Basil Blackwell.

Sweetman, Jim. 1990. *Language Links*. London: Collins.

Thiong, Ngugi wa. 1981. *Decolonizing the Mind*. London: Heinemann.

Trudgill, P. 1983. *Sociolinguistics*. Harmondsworth: Penguin.

Trudgill, P. and **J. Hannah.** 1982. *International English – a Guide to Varieties of Standard English*. London: Edward Arnold.

Widdowson, H. G. 1993. The ownership of English. The Peter Strevens Memorial Lecture, published in the IATEFL 1993 Annual Conference Report. Whitstable: IATEFL.

Williams, R. 1976. *Keywords*. London: Fontana.

Index

Index

Index

pronunciation, 7, 8
  attitudes to RP, 62–3
  see also accent
punctuation, 61

reader, as audience, 17–18, 21
Received Pronunciation, 62–3
referential knowledge, 19, 21
reflection, about language, 67–88
regional associations, 7, 34, 36, 37, 104
registers, appreciation of use, 99–100
religious English, 34
Richards, J., 99
role-play, 73–4
Romaine, S., 89

school *see* education
scientific English, 33–4
Scottish English, 30–1, 52–3
Sinclair, B., 68
speech *see* spoken language
spelling, 61
  differences, American/British English, 50–2
spoken language:
  contrast with written language, 33, 62–6
  conversational openings, analysis, 69–70
  diagnostic analysis, 90–4
  interpersonal nature, 65–6
  speech transcripts, 40
  talk, analysis (case-study), 70–3
  see also Standard Spoken English
Standard American English, 49
Standard British English, 46–9
  dialects, 56
Standard English English, 52–3
Standard Scottish English, 52–3
Standard Spoken English, 11, 35–7, 43, 104
Standard Written English, 11, 34, 36–7, 43–4
standards, social, 1, 23–5, 29–30, 44
stress, differences, American/British English, 50–2
Stubbs, M., 27–8
style, formal/informal, 100–3
superiority, of Standard English, 4, 23–4, 29, 37

syntax, and comprehension, 58

talk *see* spoken language
teaching of English:
  diagnostic analysis in, 89–98
  Standard English, 28–9, 61
  Standard Spoken English, 11, 43
  Standard Written English, 11, 43–4
  use of language, 67–8
  see also KAL; National Curriculum
technical language, 18
terminology, for description of language, 75–6
texts:
  and audience, 18–22
  distinctive forms, 84–6
Trudgill, P., 32, 54

use *see* language use

variation:
  dialectal, in British English, 53–9
  in forms of Standard Englishes, 30–7, 44, 50–3, 58–9
  in Standard English, 21, 28
vocabulary:
  comprehensibility issues, 58
  differences:
    American/British English, 50–2
    in dialect, 35
  homogeneity:
    among international Englishes, 58
    between Standard and non-Standard English, 93–4
  jargon, 42–3
  in varieties of Standard English, 33–4, 37, 42, 44
  variety-specific items, 58

Widdowson, H. G., 21, 104
Williams, R., 24
written language:
  contrast with spoken language, 11, 33, 62–6
  creative use, by writers, 59–60
  diagnostic analysis, 94–8
  and use of Standard English, 33–4, 61, 98, 99–100
  varieties, 33–4
  see also Standard Written English